As God's Witness

The Death of Knute Rockne

Jeffrey G. Harrell

Rochelle Day / Layout Designer

*Georges Toumayan / Cover
Designer & Tech Assistant
Richard T. Ryan / Editor
Len Clark / Editor*

Mato Publishing L.L.C., South Bend, Indiana

spiritofknute.com

*Library of Congress Cataloging-in-Publication
Data is available upon request.

eBook - ISBN 978 1-64921-679-3

Print - ISBN 978 1-64921-677-9

PRINTED IN THE UNITED STATES OF AMERICA

Book design by Rochelle Day

Jacket design by Georges Toumayan

First Edition: May 2020

CONTENTS

Authors'

Introduction

When the country lost Knute Rockne, the world lost an amazing man.

Knute (Ka-noot) Rockne, the Norwegian immigrant and part-time chemistry professor who shaped the game of football as a player and a coach at the University of Notre Dame in the early 20th century.... and, literally, the ball itself.

The football legend known simply to his friends as "Rock" established Notre Dame as a cornerstone of American college football during an epic head coaching career that began at old Cartier Field in 1918 and ended in the iconic stadium that Rockne himself built, Notre Dame Stadium, with a third national championship in 1930.

"As God's Witness" picks up less than a year before Knute Rockne was killed in a plane crash in a remote Kansas pasture at about 10:45 a.m. on March 31, 1931.

Pieced together from more than 100 time-period newspaper articles through newspaperarchives.com; the U.S. Department of Commerce's official crash investigation report; books detailing the Chicago mob, the life of Al Capone, and the infamous murder of Chicago Tribune reporter Jake Lingle, "As God's Witness" is the first historical account to thoroughly explore the circumstances leading up to the fateful plane crash that ended the highly-public life of one of America's greatest sports icons.

What begins with the hit on Lingle in a downtown Chicago train station on June 9, 1930 expands through the Notre Dame priest who swapped his plane ticket with his friend Rockne the day after he had testified in the trial of a Capone hitman charged in the Lingle murder.

It's been 90 years since Jake Lingle whispered his dying confession into the ear of Father John Reynolds as he lay on the ground of the Randolph Street Train Station with a bullet in his head. It's been 34 years since Father Reynolds last spoke about being the only direct eyewitness to the Jake Lingle murder and defying mob intimidation to testify in a trial that only Father Reynolds knew had convicted the wrong man.

It's as if Father Reynolds is telling his story for the first time "As God's Witness."

South Bend, Indiana
March 31, 2020

Prologue

Knute Rockne was beat up.

Going into the 1930 season, his 13th as head coach of the University of Notre Dame, Rockne's worn-out body moved delicately on a pair of wobbly legs nearly crippled by phlebitis.

Twelve grueling years racing non-stop around the clock coaching the best college football team in the land had finally caught up with the legend in his own time. No coach, not Glenn "Pop" Warner, not Amos Alonzo Stagg, not even Walter Camp, who was widely considered to be the most important figure in the earliest development of American football, worked as tirelessly as Rockne to build the game for the future.

It was Rockne who had perfected the forward pass. It was Rockne who had devised the pre-snap shift. It was Rockne who had installed the first complex passing system to complement the running game. It was Rockne who not only shaped the modern ball, but designed it with laces and a valve to regulate air pressure so it fit comfortably in the quarterback's hand for passing.

Rockne built the Notre Dame Fighting Irish football team into a national institution and singlehandedly sold the college football game to an entire nation. Rockne designed and built the 54,000-seat football mecca known as Notre Dame Stadium, a college football hub that has since been expanded several times and now holds more than 80,000 fans.

There was Babe Ruth…and there was Knute Rockne.

All the other superstars of the '20s – Red Grange, Jack Dempsey, even presidents Warren G. Harding and Herbert Hoover – paled in their larger-than-life shadows. And not even the mighty Ruth could match the visionary intellect of Rockne.

There weren't enough hours in the year to keep up with Rockne's grueling schedule. He oversaw the business end of his own line of sporting goods, including his new streamlined football, which was sold nationally through Wilson Sporting Goods. He was the face of the Studebaker Corp., traveling relentlessly to cities across the country, motivating the South Bend-based automobile manufacturer's sales forces with the same charismatic flair he used to fire up his teams.

The pay from Studebaker, $10,000, far outweighed the $125-per-20-minute-talk fee Rockne had received from the Leigh-Emmerich lecture firm in New York. But with the higher salary came a relentless travel schedule that took Rockne from coast to coast all winter long from 1928 into 1929, and stretched into football season.

When the National Association of Finance Companies contacted Rockne to address its annual convention in 1929,

Rockne did not respond, prompting the NAFC to ask Studebaker President Albert Erskine to intercede and persuade the Notre Dame coach to appear. Erskine also headed up Notre Dame's lay board of trustees and was a prominent patron of the university – and to its' head football coach.

Erskine forwarded the association's letter to Rockne with an appended note: "Dear Rock. It's worth $300 if you want it." Rockne took the money and made the trip to Chicago to speak to the convention.

In addition to a relentless lecture circuit, Rockne also entertained frequent offers to work in Hollywood on movies. At 42, however, Rockne's health had deteriorated severely; the Notre Dame football coach was in danger of dropping dead on the spot.

The previous season had been hell on Rockne. Having all four wisdom teeth pulled at the same time exacerbated a series of nagging ailments. Then, immediately after the Fighting Irish shut down Indiana 14-0 in the 1929 opener, Rockne was forced to his bed with a serious illness that threatened to keep him from traveling with the team to Baltimore for an important matchup against rival Navy.

That week Rockne lay in bed perusing the book "Gray's Anatomy," it hit him what might have knocked him down. "Doc," Rockne said in a phone call to his personal physician Dr. C.J. Barborka, "I think I have phlebitis."

Only Rockne could have diagnosed himself with such a complicated and debilitating attack on his body. Graduating from Notre Dame in 1914, Rockne had every intention of moving to St. Louis to study medicine and pay his way through St. Louis University Medical School coaching football on the side. But when St. Louis Medical School administrators insisted his plate would be filled with a med student's curriculum that would leave little time for extra hours to coach football, Rockne decided his best interests would be served by remaining in South Bend.

Dr. Barborka agreed with Rockne's assessment. Thrombophlebitis, an inflammation of the veins in his legs, would keep Rockne bedridden. The doctor also advised Rockne to rest quietly and stay calm. Excitement could cause a blood clot in his legs to dislodge and launch into his blood stream, creating the potential for a fatal heart attack or stroke.

But the Norway-born Rockne was the legendary "Rock," tough as leather, fiercely competitive, the unequivocal Viking of college football coaches. "Can't" was not in his vocabulary. Not even a life-threatening condition could keep him away for the game against Carnegie Tech, a middle-of-the-road group that had embarrassed Rockne's Fighting Irish the previous year in Notre Dame's final game at old Cartier Field – the only loss the Fighting Irish suffered in the 23-year history of Cartier Field.

In the locker room under Pittsburgh's Forbes Field before the game, the door flew open and interim coach Tom Lieb burst in to stun Rockne's Ramblers with Rockne in his arms. Team physician Dr. Maurice Kelly stood awestruck and shocked in a corner.

"If he lets go," Dr. Kelly said to a man next to him, "and that clot dislodges to his heart or to his brain, he's got an even-chance of never leaving this dressing room alive."

Rockne stood in the middle of the locker room surrounded by his team. As he began to speak to his players in a quiet, determined tone, his voice grew louder and clearer as if each word were a sail catching the tail wind of an ocean squall.

"A lot of water has gone under the bridge since I first came to Notre Dame, but I don't know if I've ever wanted to win a game as badly as this one," Rockne pleaded in his demanding metallic, nasal call to arms that could drive a group of men into a fiery inferno with no thought other than coming out wet with victory.

"I don't care what happens after today. Why do you think I'm taking a chance like this? To see you lose? They'll be primed. They'll be tough. They think they have your number. Are you going to let it happen again?"

Each member of the team hung on every word as if it were Rockne's last.

"We will probably win the toss. I want you in run down the field and tackle them and go on the defensive. Stop them dead and take the heart out of them! You men in the backfield, be alert, heads up, smart; look for that ball when they throw a pass, and when they do, go in and get the ball.

"I want you to block as you never blocked before; I want you to do as well, as hard, as mechanically perfect as you can think of. And the quarterback thinks clearly and calls the right play. And you men, all eleven of you dig those cleats in deep, get your jaws set and when you start for that goal line, drive, drive, drive!

"Go out there and crack 'em. Crack 'em. Crack 'em. Fight to live. Fight to win. Fight to live. Fight to win... win... WIN!"

They did win, in a dogfight that ended 7-0. After the game, the battered team and their ailing coach returned to South Bend.

Rockne's condition refused to subside just as stubbornly as his fierce nature refused to give in to bed rest. The rest of the season, Rockne attended the games, and coached, from a wheelchair, traveling to other schools to play "home games" while the new Notre Dame Stadium that Rockne had fought bitterly with the school's ruling Holy Cross fathers to build was under construction.

At practice, Rockne sat in the backseat of a car and shouted out instructions over a public address system designed specifically for his weakened voice by Lou Burroughs and Albert R. Kahn, a pair of audio manufacturers whose company, Radio Engineers, serviced radio receivers in the basement of the Century Tire and Rubber Company in South Bend. Rockne dubbed the system his "electric voice," a moniker that inspired the name of the company that continues to produce microphones and PA systems today – "Electro-Voice."

Frank Leahy had dislocated his elbow during the Navy game. With family coming to the game against the University of Southern California at Soldier Field in Chicago, Leahy badly wanted to play. Besides, Leahy reasoned, "If (Rockne) could risk his life, why couldn't I play football with a dislocated elbow?"

Doctors removed Leahy's cast on orders not to do anything foolish. When he came off the practice field, Rockne got out of the car and approached Leahy with the question: "How's the elbow?"

"Couldn't be better," Leahy replied.

"In that case, let's see you flex it," Rockne commanded.

Realizing that Rockne had not been at the Navy game, Leahy figured Rockne did not know that he had injured his right elbow. He produced his left arm, moved it up and down, made motions like a baseball pitcher stretching, and won Rockne's green light to order interim Head Coach Tom Lieb to use Leahy at right tackle. Rockne probably wouldn't be at the USC game, anyway, Leahy assumed.

He assumed wrong.

Leahy, predictably, re-injured his elbow during the first half of the USC game. He was lying on the training table at halftime when the door swung open and Rockne appeared, pale and frightfully frail in a wheelchair. Rockne tried to stand, but his legs couldn't hold him and he fell backwards. Leahy leaped off the table and stood in the doorway to watch as Rockne held up his chin as high as he could, and, in a weakened voice that barely resembled his usually-powerful staccato, launched into a speech that made the Gipper rally cry sound like idle chit-chat.

"Boys, get out there and play them hard the first five minutes," Rockne beckoned. "They'll hate it, but play them hard. Rock will be upstairs watching you. Go ahead now.

Hit them hard. Win! Win! Win! That's the only reason for playing. Crack 'em! Crack 'em! I'll be watching!"

It took a trainer to hold Leahy back from jumping in line with the rest of his teammates to hit the field for the second half. When it was over, Notre Dame had beaten USC for its seventh straight victory of the year.

Later in the week after the USC game, Curly Lambeau, the founder of the Green Bay Packers who had played at Notre Dame in 1918 during Rockne's first year as head coach, approached his former mentor to see how he was doing.

"What kind of team you got?" Lambeau asked.

"Best damn team I ever had," Rockne answered. "But I can't tell them that."

"Why?" Lambeau inquired.

"They might believe me," Rockne replied.

The end of the 1929 season saw the Fighting Irish finish 9-0, their fifth undefeated season under his lead. Rockne was a national championship coach for the second time, the first one coming in 1924.

When January 1930 rolled in, Rockne flew to Florida to take a welcomed family vacation in Miami with his wife, Bonnie, and his four kids – Knute Jr., Bill, Mary Jeanne, and the youngest, Jackie.

His health, particularly his legs, remained shaky. He planned a visit with one of his former players – Charlie Bachman, who was head coach at the University of Florida – during a stopover in Jacksonville on his way to Miami. But Rockne wrote Bachman a letter saying the visit had to be delayed.

"Did not wire you to meet me at Jacksonville as I could not get out of the berth anyway," Rockne wrote. "Is there any chance for you to drop down here? We have a great plan for me to sort of vegetate. Will drive up in our car just as soon as I can travel. Have lots of football I have to go over with you..."

The Florida vacation agreed with Rockne. He returned home to South Bend before catching a flight in March to the West Coast to conduct business for Studebaker in Los Angeles. He also took time to travel to Seattle, Washington, to partake in one of his favorite leisure activities: golf.

Football would remain on hiatus when he returned to South Bend. Again, Rockne was forced to summon Dr. Barborka, who diagnosed the coach with a severe case of bronchitis. Rockne laid low for a few weeks, then caught a train to Rochester, Minnesota, where he wound up being admitted to the Mayo Clinic.

By mid-May, Rockne was back home on Notre Dame's campus. His faltering health prompted letters to Bachman and a handful of other coaching pals informing them that he needed to meet and get their advice. The meeting, he wrote, would be held at 1 p.m. on May 31, "... to discuss the problem which affects all of us very vitally."

Rockne was not only ill in May, 1930, he was too exhausted to catch his breath from a vacation. The coach was only 42 years old, but hidden underneath that rugged bald head and pug-nose prizefighter's mug was the body of a worn-out 72-year-old.

The meeting with his closest coaching confidants called for a heartfelt discussion over whether Rockne would be able to lead the Notre Dame Fighting Irish for a 13th season.

Nine days after that May 31, 1930 meeting at Notre Dame, Rockne traveled to Chicago to attend the Ninth Annual Collegiate Track and Field Championships at the University of Chicago's Stagg Field.

The field's namesake, Amos Alonzo Stagg, had served as a mentor to Rockne since the landmark Chicago football and track coach had recognized the teenager as one of the kids sucking wind under the stands after ducking out of a marathon race early. It was a good day for Rockne to take in the collegiate track championships with the coach who had served as a beloved father figure – and to discuss his health and coaching plans with one of his most revered advisors.

Just a few short miles north of the South 57th Street stadium up Lake Shore Drive, a series of events began swirling around the corner of Randolph Street and Michigan Avenue in downtown Chicago that would determine the fate of Knute Kenneth Rockne.

Section 1: The Hit

1

A TAIL ON JAKE LINGLE

The loud blast of a car horn startled pedestrians in their tracks as they strolled along Randolph Street under a clear blue downtown Chicago sky during the early afternoon of June 9, 1930.

Jake Lingle left his plush residential suite at the Stevens Hotel around noon and walked a mile-and-a-half to the Tribune Tower to meet with the city editor at The Chicago Tribune. The Tribune's top street reporter was on the trail of a story surrounding a murdered body found a couple of days ago and needed to discuss rumors of a brewing gangland riff with his boss.

With business for the day concluded and now on his way to catch the 1:30 p.m. train to the horse track, Lingle unwrapped one of the cigars he had purchased from the

Sherman Hotel's kiosk. He buried his head in the Daily Racing Form he had picked up from the newsstand in front of the public library and made his way south across Wacker Drive toward the suburban station of the Illinois Central Railroad at the corner of Randolph Street and Michigan Avenue.

The deafening blast of the horn about 50 feet way away startled Lingle.

"Play Hy Schneider in the third!" a booming voice shouted through the open window of a car that had rolled up on the south side of Randolph. Lingle caught the eyes of two men sitting in a roadster.

"I've got him," Lingle replied with a grin and a slight wave.

Two other men on foot suddenly appeared from the shadows of a back alley and flanked Lingle from behind. One was tall, decked out in a gray suit with light hair showing from the bottom edge of a straw boater: He had just emerged from a public restroom where he had taken a hit of a powdery drug to relax his shaky nerves. The other was a shorter, stocky figure with black glossy hair slicked back on his head.

Lingle was oblivious. His eyes scoured the racing form for the day's potential winners. He walked four blocks to Michigan Avenue, then continued toward the subway station, head buried in the racing form. Entering the station, Lingle proceeded downstairs to the underground walkway leading to the Illinois Central suburban electric railroad in Grant Park.

The two men tailed Lingle step-for-step, hiding in plain sight. The subway station was too packed with afternoon shoppers and office workers for anyone to stand out. The two men were fixated on Lingle. They didn't as much as peek away from their target when the screeching brakes of an arriving train filled with passengers from South Bend reverberated loudly throughout the station.

Former Chicago Coroner's Physician Dr. Joseph Springer spotted his longtime friend Lingle walking a short distance away. Lingle didn't look up from his racing form. Springer saw two men walking suspiciously close to Lingle as he made his way into the underground subway station, but the doctor figured they were part of the afternoon rush.

Lingle came to a halt about 25 feet from the east exit. The dark-haired man slowed, took a few steps back, then paused at the sight of a priest stepping off the train. The priest walked toward Lingle and both men on the train platform.

Lingle looked up and spotted the priest's white collar. He smiled and waved. His eyes were hopeful a return wave from the priest would bless him with good luck later at the track.

The priest returned the nod. Lingle took it as a sign from above that it was going to be his lucky day.

2

PATH OF A MOB REPORTER

Nobody ever confused Alfred "Jake" Lingle with Ernie Pyle, Grantland Rice, or even a janitor sweeping the newsroom at the Chicago Tribune.

Solidly built of medium height with curly black hair and a prominent cleft on the bottom of a moony face that emitted a self-satisfied smirk of cynical boyish charm, Lingle married his childhood sweetheart, Helen Sullivan, and the couple raised two children born a year apart, Alfred Jr. and Dolores. Lingle held true to his marriage vows. He was a faithful husband who limited his drinking to a glass or two of beer, largely because of a stomach ulcer.

The streets of Chicago were Lingle's office. A bona fide "legman" reporter with a grade school education who started at the Chicago Tribune as a 20-year-old office boy in 1912, Lingle never staked claim to a byline. He wasn't illiterate, but he had no interest in culture, and he probably never read more than a half-dozen books. When it came to writing simple English, he couldn't, which was why Lingle's name was virtually unknown to Tribune readers.

Lingle earned $65 a week working under the title of "reporter" at the Tribune, although he never typed a word, had no interest in reading writers who wrote them, and only stepped inside the building that housed the prominent Chicago Tribune newspaper to meet with an editor or collect his paycheck.

Lingle's gift was an uncanny ability to blend into the streets and back alleys of Chicago's toughest core and dig up stories from the underground whispers of a wide spectrum of sources. Everybody knew Lingle, and Lingle knew everybody – from hotel clerks, bookies, gambling house owners and bootleggers to the highest order of Chicago's power elite on both sides of the law, spanning police ranks, judges, lawyers, prosecutors and politicians, including the city's two high lords of crime, Al Capone and George "Bugs" Moran.

Instead of writing, Lingle relentlessly plied his trade on the phone. Story after story, scoop after scoop was called into the Tribune's city editor's desk then turned over to the paper's rewrite men. Jake Lingle was the Tribune's house crime expert, the paper's golden goose, the bridge between the streets and the actual writers who turned the deepest, darkest secrets of Chicago's underworld into the light that shined from front-page headlines on the crime story of the day.

The $65-a-week Lingle pulled from the Tribune was chump change, a legitimate paycheck that kept the eyes of the IRS off the massive flow of cash he piled up moonlighting as a bagman on the payroll of Al Capone. Along with gathering street chatter to phone in to the Tribune's city editors, Lingle delivered payments from Capone's Cicero headquarters to crooked politicians and judges to the tune of an estimated $60,000 a year.

Balancing enormous press clout with gangland street influence gave Lingle money to burn. He owned a Lincoln car with a chauffeur. He plunged on the stock market. He hit the horse track daily during the season in pursuit of his lone vice, gambling, sometimes laying as much as $1,000 down on a horse race but never betting less than $100.

Lingle took care of his wife and two children handsomely by providing them with a lavish apartment on Chicago's West Side. When he worked the streets, Lingle resided at the best hotels, most notably a suite of apartments at the plush Stevens Hotel on Michigan Avenue where the switchboard operator had orders never to disturb him unless the caller's name appeared on the list Lingle had provided.

When he needed to get away from the city, Lingle stayed at a posh $25,000 Lake Michigan-front summer home he owned on the "Michigan Riviera" at Long Beach, Indiana. Winter vacations were spent a month at a time in Havana, Cuba, where Lingle made sure every bookmaker at the race track and every dealer at the gambling tables knew when he was in town.

He hobnobbed with millionaires. Dined at the most expensive restaurants. Smoked 50-cent cigars. Rubbed elbows with the governor of Illinois, the state's attorney general, judges, and county and city officials of Chicago's political machine. Lingle golfed, vacationed, and became close personal friends with Chicago Police Commissioner William P. Russell.

Then there was Al Capone.

Lingle stood in high favor with Capone, and neither made an attempt to conceal the friendship in public. It was not unusual for Lingle to be seen hanging out at Capone's headquarters at the Hawthorne Inn in Cicero. Nor was Capone shy about welcoming Lingle into his home near Miami on several occasions. One of Lingle's favorite gifts to flaunt was a belt with a diamond-studded buckle given to him by Capone.

"A Christmas present," Capone admitted. "Jake was a dear friend of mine."

Lingle's tight relationship with Capone afforded him an open understanding to work Chicago's streets on both sides of the law – and both sides of town between Capone's South Side and Moran's North Side operations. He once bragged that his friendship with Capone had allowed him to "fix the price of beer" in Chicago.

His personal finances were top secret, however. A secret account Lingle kept with the Lake Shore Trust and Savings Bank lined his pockets with a perpetual wad of cash. Collaborating on an investment partnership with his pal, Police Commissioner William Russell – a joint securities account opened in November 1928 with a

$20,000 deposit – remained as hushed as an FBI investigation.

Not that Lingle possessed keen financial vision. Had Lingle liquidated his securities at the height of a bull market in September 1929, he would have turned a profit of $85,000. Instead, he held on, and a month later Black Thursday rang in the Great Depression. Lingle's and Russell's profits evaporated, along with an additional $75,000.

Lingle showed losses of more than $200,000 on paper. But rather than lower his standard of living, the river of cash flowing in daily from his underworld business connections afforded Lingle the luxury of elevating his lifestyle with a slew of deposits into Lake Shore Trust and Savings, totaling nearly $64,000 between the end of 1929 and the spring of 1930.

The deposits, and Lingle's lavish lifestyle, were not lost on his bosses and colleagues at the Chicago Tribune, although none of his Tribune associates viewed Lingle's gangland relationships as anything other than the good cultivation of news sources. Lingle lied that his father had bequeathed him $11,000 when in fact his father left only $500 in a will. He also fibbed about the value of some of his stocks tripling during the bull market. In fact, Lingle and Russell had been wiped out. None of Lingle's Tribune colleagues was aware that he was brazenly taking loans from gamblers, politicians, businessmen, mobsters, anybody who would pay him to curry a favor using his enormous press clout.

Lingle always took the money. Rarely, if ever, did he pay anybody back.

Lingle borrowed $2,000 from Jimmy Mondi, a Capone gambling operator in Cicero and downtown in the Loop – a loan that was never repaid. Another $5,000 borrowed from Alderman Berthold A. Cronson was never paid back. Loans of $2,500 from Carlos Ames, president of the Civil Service Commission; $300 from police Lt. Thomas McFarland; $20,000 from roadhouse and gambling parlor operator Sam Hare – all suffered the same fate.

Yet Lingle continued to survive with his knees and limbs intact. His good health was much more valuable to Chicago's underworld and the city's political machine because his citywide influence generated money. Stories were "planted" in the Tribune on Capone's behalf. Law enforcement connections were engaged to tip off Capone about impending police raids on the gangster's bootlegging and other illegal activities. Lingle could easily "put the fix in" for gamblers, bootleggers and anyone else who was having a problem with law enforcement.

Once, Lingle negotiated his position as Tribune reporter to spy for Capone on rival Bugs Moran's North Side Gang. That effort helped Capone and his crew block Moran's efforts to muscle in on Capone's territory.

Lingle's tight bonds with Chicago police and Capone put him on the right side of perhaps gangland's most prolific power play, the St. Valentine's Day Massacre.

At 10:30 a.m. on Feb. 14, 1929, seven members and associates of Moran's North Side Gang were lined up against a wall inside a garage at 2122 North Clark Street and mowed down in a heavy blaze of Thompson submachine gun fire.

The four executioners were never identified. But the suspects were rumored to be former members of the Egan's Rats, a notorious organized crime gang in St. Louis named for mobster Tom Egan who co-formed what became feared as the city's worst political terrorists. All four hitmen were working on the orders of Capone with inside help from members of the Chicago Police Department avenging the killing of a police officer's son. Two of the shooters wore suits, ties, overcoats and hats, while the other two were dressed as uniformed policemen.

Moran was the prime target. Capone's main rival avoided the slaughter when he showed up at the garage early, saw nobody there, then drove away. Afterwards, Capone allowed Moran to live and continue to operate his business on the North Side as long as Capone got his cut of the action. It became crystal clear to everyone on the streets that there was only one crime boss calling the shots in Chicago.

By 1930, the protective wall put up around Lingle by Capone began to crumble. Too many loans taken in return for favors that weren't paid back were piling up on Lingle's tab. His street cred on both sides of the law suffered when he got too deeply involved in the struggle for money and power in the city's gambling syndicate. Lingle may have been the resident "gangologist" at the Tribune, but out on the street he was a "favor seller" whose word was getting cheaper by the day.

Lingle took one step closer to the morgue the day he was given $50,000 by Capone to secure protection for a West Side dog track. As he had done so many times before with loans, Lingle failed to follow through and kept the money. Except this wasn't some low-level street gambler trying to buy favor through Lingle's press influence... this was Al Capone.

The noose tightened when Lingle got involved with the re-opening of the Sheridan Wave Tournament Club, an elegant society gambling parlor on Waveland Avenue under the protection of Moran's North Siders before it shut down in the wake of the St. Valentine's Day Massacre. In its heyday, the club was the ritziest casino in the city and perhaps the entire country, a social hub for the city's fashionable clientele who enjoyed food, drink, women and whatever else they wanted on the house, and enriched the owners by tens of thousands of dollars each night.

Moran took 25 percent of the gross from the Sheridan Wave Tournament Club. Lingle's cut was 10 percent.

Moran worked for 18 months trying to persuade sympathetic city officials to help him reopen the Sheridan Wave Tournament Club. With city approvals in hand, Moran brought in Joe Josephs and Julian "Potatoes" Kaufman, an old friend of Lingle's, to manage the club. Kaufman approached Lingle and asked if he could use his influence with the police department to get the club reopened.

"You'll be satisfied, of course," Kaufman pitched with a rhetorical question, "with the 10 percent cut you got before?"

"Not by a damned sight," Lingle shot back. "I want 50 percent this time."

"But we have to pay Bugs Moran 25 percent," Kaufman reasoned.

"To hell with Bugs Moran," Lingle huffed.

"Well," Kaufman insisted, "Bugs is the boss of the North Side. You know that. We couldn't do business unless he said the word."

Fully aware that nobody did underworld business in Chicago without Capone's word, Lingle puffed his chest out and refused to back down.

"Moran cuts no ice with the police nowadays. He's on the blacklist," Lingle said. "Give him the air and put me on your payroll for his cut. I'll do the protecting, and I want 50 percent for doing it."

Kaufman couldn't believe his ears. He bumped his offer up to 15 percent.

"Fifty percent or you don't run," Lingle replied.

Kaufman's tone flared angrily.

"Say, Lingle, who do you think you are? A mob all by yourself? You're getting the swell-head. You can't put any such stuff over on me. I'm no sucker. There'll be nothing doing on any 50 percent for you. And I'll open, too. You can bet your shirt on that."

Lingle remained cocky.

"Come through with my 50 percent," he fired back. "Or on opening night you'll see more squad cars full of coppers at your door than you ever saw before in your life."

Under the cloud of Lingle's threat, the club was set to reopen on June 9. But Kaufman couldn't bring Lingle in. The doors would stay shut.

Moran was furious.

Lingle's buddy, Capone, was livid.

3

KILLERS IN A SUBWAY

T he night before the scheduled reopening of the
Sheridan Wave Tournament Club, Lingle made his way
over to Randolph Street in the Loop to meet with one of his
most knowledgeable sources, attorney Louis B. Piquett.

Piquett, a former bartender who studied law in night
school, landed his first job as chief clerk to the city
prosecutor of Chicago largely because of his prolific
activism in Chicago Democratic politics. Political
networking didn't keep Piquett from being indicted on
corruption charges in 1923 – not long after he had been
appointed city prosecutor by Mayor William Hale
Thompson. After the charges were dropped, Piquett left the
prosecutor's office and entered private practice in 1923. He
had carved out a lucrative law business defending

Chicago's underworld by being the first set of ears to hear every truth behind every dead body found on the streets of Chicago.

Piquett, one of the Lingle's most valuable sources, had information on a murder victim, Red McLaughlin, a known mob acquaintance whose body had been found in a canal.

As Lingle stood on the sidewalk discussing the murder with Piquett, a blue sedan with two men inside pulled up and stopped at the curb. Lingle spotted the car out of the corner of his eye. He cut the conversation off in mid-sentence, told Piquett goodbye, then abruptly ducked into a nearby store.

The next morning, Lingle walked to the Tribune offices and met briefly with the city editor over rumors of a gang beef that had caused McLaughlin to wind up with a bullet in his head.

With an hour to spare before the 1:30 p.m. train left for Washington Park horse track in Homewood, Lingle stopped in at the Sherman Hotel's coffee shop for a bite to eat. Standing at the counter when he walked in was his friend, police Sgt. Tom Alcock of the Detective Bureau.

"I'm being tailed." Lingle's nonchalance in recounting the shadowy encounter with Piquett the night before gave Alcock reason to shrug the claim off as idle chatter.

A few minutes later while walking on Randolph Street toward the subway, Lingle heard the call, "Play Hy Schneider in the third!" coming from a car carrying two men that had pulled up within earshot on the south side of the street.

"I've got him," Lingle called back.

Lingle was oblivious to the fact that he had just been fingered for two hitmen on foot.

Before reaching the subway, Lingle stopped about 25 feet from the east exit. The dark-haired man slowed and took a few cautionary steps back. Lingle had noticed a priest walking from the train platform.

He smiled and waved at the priest.

The priest returned Lingle's wave with a nod that took his eyes directly into the stark gaze of a dark-haired figure looking to see who Lingle was waving to.

In clear view of the priest, the man in the hat stepped directly behind Lingle. He pulled a snub-nosed .38 Colt from his waistband, but his drugged nerves got the better of him and he clumsily fumbled the gun.

The dark-haired man quickly snatched the weapon from his accomplice. The priest stood motionless; his eyes fixed on the surreal sequence of events happening directly in front of him.

The gunman lifted the barrel of the .38 to the back of Lingle's head. The gun exploded with a single blast that echoed through the subway station.

The bullet powered upward into Lingle's brain and exited through his forehead. Lingle lurched forward, still clutching the racing form in his hands. The train that would've taken the Tribune reporter to the horse track pulled into the subway station right on time. Lingle lied on the ground bleeding profusely, a cigar tightly clenched in his teeth.

Stunned passengers poured out of the train and scattered over the chaotic platform. The gunman tossed the gun to the side and ran into the crowd to blend in before police could reach the fallen victim.

Bystander Patrick Campbell noticed the dark-haired gunman hurrying away and took off in pursuit.

The priest moved swiftly toward the dying body. He knelt next to the gravely injured Lingle to administer last rites. Lingle whispered into the priest's ear.

He took one final breath…

Jake Lingle died with his head cradled in the priest's arms.

The blond suspect unwittingly doubled back past Lingle's body and ran up the staircase. Reaching the top of the stairs, he jumped a fence, but altered his direction and took off running west on Randolph Street. With police in full pursuit with guns drawn, the suspect tossed off a left-handed silk glove and scampered onto Wabash Avenue. He disappeared into the dense sidewalk crowd of downtown Chicago.

The priest released Lingle. He stood, started to run off but bumped into Campbell, obstructing the path Campbell was clearing in his attempt to run down the dark-haired gunman, who by now had disappeared into the crowd.

"Somebody has been shot, I'm getting upstairs to see what is going on!" the priest shouted to Campbell. Chicago Police Lt. William Cusack of the Detective Bureau heard the exchange.

"He was no priest," the police lieutenant barked as the priest fled in another direction. "A priest would never do that. He would have gone to the side of the stricken person."

The detective never saw the priest stop to administer last rites to the dying Lingle.

4

FATHER REYNOLDS

John Joseph Reynolds came into this world in Brooklyn, New York, in 1894, the son of Thomas Reynolds, an engineer on the ferry boat that connected New York City and New Jersey, and Elizabeth Reynolds, the mother Johnnie Reynolds would lose at the age of 6 to brain cancer.

Unable to raise three young boys and a girl on his own, Thomas Reynolds sent his children to an orphanage in Brooklyn. When details were worked out with the orphanage, the siblings found homes with family members in Thomas Reynolds' hometown of Bellows Falls, Vermont, a small village in the town of Rockingham that served as home to the Boston & Maine Railroad.

Johnnie had difficulty with losing his mother at such a young age and being farmed out to an orphanage by his father. At the orphanage Johnnie was constantly getting into fights over anything that triggered his temper, even when somebody made fun of his Brooklyn accent. He was the last of his siblings to find a home because he was too hard to handle

Only one relative in Bellows Falls was equipped to deal with Johnnie and raise the mad-as-hell child with a hair-trigger temper and quicker fists as a son: The Rev. Edward Reynolds, C.S.C., pulled his nephew out of the orphanage and took him into the home where he served as parish priest of Bellows Falls.

Father Edward Reynolds was kind, patient, and tough as nails which earned him the respect of the local townsfolk. Bellows Falls was home to the railroad and a paper mill, both of which were rife with union activities. Father Edward was counted on to act as the town's tough-minded peace-keeper whenever the threat of a union strike surfaced, a community service that won him significant influence with the hierarchy of the paper mill.

But Johnnie was a handful. Despite his small wiry size, he could be a dynamite blast even for Father Edward. Johnnie took on any kid in the neighborhood. Any adult. Any time. Any place. Anywhere. Johnnie's rage didn't need a reason. Once, when he was 12, a teacher attempted to dish out a dose of discipline with a ruler. Every time the teacher hit him, Johnnie fought for the ruler and tried to hit her back.

"I licked every kid in town because they made fun of my Brooklyn accent," Johnnie would boast.

By the time Johnnie entered Bellows Falls High School, teenage maturity had mellowed him into the makings of a popular student. He excelled in the classroom, and friends came easier as his athletic prowess began to shine brightly. Johnnie developed into a prolific runner, a star on the track team who specialized in the 2-mile run.

But there was still the occasional fight. A friend, Owen Murphy, punched Johnnie in the nose during horseplay one afternoon. Murphy was left with a broken thumb from the fight. Johnnie took a shot to the nose that left him with a deviated septum and severe sinus problems that would plague him the rest of his life.

Although located halfway across the country from South Bend, Bellows Falls was a mere six degrees of separation from Notre Dame. Owen Murphy's family was related to the O'Conner family, which produced Paul "Bucky" O'Conner, a star Bellows Falls High School athlete who would go on to play running back at Notre Dame under Knute Rockne in the coach's last national championship season.

By the time Johnnie graduated from Bellows Falls High School in 1912, he was practically running the parish for his uncle. Father Edward offered to help his 19-year-old nephew get a good job in the office at the local paper mill where his union peacekeeping efforts had earned him enormous influence.

"Or," Father Edward suggested, "if you want to be a priest, I'll send you to Notre Dame. They have a good English course there."

Johnnie had to get out of Bellows Falls. Notre Dame offered the perfect landing spot where he could study for the priesthood at Holy Cross seminary. With his uncle's blessing, Johnnie headed to South Bend to enter the seminary and study English.

He also planned to join the track team; a squad coached by 27-year-old Knute Rockne. Rockne's coaching career at Notre Dame would be bookended by a pair of Bellows Falls High School students – Johnnie Reynolds, a Notre Dame track star who set a national record for the 2-mile run in 1916; and Bucky O'Connor, a third-string running back who would rush for 142 yards and lead the Fighting Irish to Rockne's last championship during the final game of the 1930 season against USC.

Johnnie Reynolds ran track, studied English and history, and became fast friends and drinking buddies with his track coach. Rockne liked tough kids and Johnnie was as tough as anybody on the track team. Despite sinus problems from all the punches he took growing up, Johnnie Reynolds picked up a prolific smoking habit.

"They bothered me, but I kept on smoking," Reynolds said of his chronic sinuses. "I had more fun smoking than I had trouble with the sinuses."

Johnnie Reynolds graduated with an A.B. degree from Notre Dame in 1916 and planned to go right into Holy Cross Seminary to pursue his studies for the priesthood. Upon graduation, the words written under his photo in the

Notre Dame yearbook described a mature young man that few back in Bellows Falls would have recognized.

"This year his thirst for knowledge and for the things beyond directed him to enter Holy Cross Seminary. He is a conscientious student and Father Oswald says that he is a professional acrobat in Greek and Latin. His quiet unpretentious manner and good nature cause him to part, in June, with a host of classmates who regard him as a scholarly gentleman and true friend."

John Joseph Reynolds was ordained a priest in 1922. The Rev. John J. Reynolds, C.S.C., briefly taught American History at Notre Dame, then moved to Portland, Oregon, where he was appointed administrator at Portland Prep School. Under Father Reynolds' leadership, Portland Prep School evolved into Portland Junior College, an evolution that would eventually expand into a full-fledged university, the University of Portland.

In 1927, Father Reynolds left Portland and returned to the University of Notre Dame to teach American history. His residence was at Morrissey Hall, and he was the assigned rector at St. Edward's Hall, supervising several members of the football team among the student residents.

While Father Reynolds was out west, his pal Knute Rockne spent seven years singlehandedly turning Notre Dame into a household name and selling the school's football program to a mass audience from coast to coast. A national schedule stretched from Army in the East to the University of Southern California on the West Coast. Upon Father Reynolds' return to South Bend, he quickly reunited with his old track coach "Rock" – now the most famous football coach in America – over beers, cigars and stories.

Johnnie Reynolds had come full circle. The angry youngster from Bellows Falls had grown into a respected Notre Dame priest and intellectual professor of American history. But Father Reynolds wasn't about to shed Johnnie from his mindset. The priest maintained an unbridled streak of character that wasn't afraid to experience life on its own terms.

On his off days, Father Reynolds caught the South Shore train to Chicago, sometimes to see his doctor for his sinus problems, sometimes to hit the horse tracks, sometimes to visit his two brothers – Edward and Thomas — both of whom lived in the city. Thomas Reynolds worked at the luxurious Edgewater Beach Hotel on the North Side near Wrigley Field, the site of the infamous shooting of baseball player Eddie Waitkus in 1949 by a 19-year-old female fan that would serve as the inspiration for the book and later the movie, "The Natural."

Johnnie Reynolds embraced Chicago. He was small in stature, 5-feet-6 maybe, but walked around with a natural street sense that came out through a quick-witted tone that often emphasized his words with a conclusive, "see." The white-collar Father Reynolds wore as a Catholic priest did not prevent Johnnie Reynolds from straying into the occasional backroom card game. Nor did the Notre Dame priest shy from getting up close and personal with the ins and outs of the horse track.

5

GOD'S WITNESS

Seeing the victim lying on the ground bleeding profusely from the head, Father Reynolds hurried to the mortally wounded man just in time to attempt to administer last rites. The man was barely able to whisper in the priest's ear before he took his final breath.

Only Father Reynolds knew the words the fallen victim had whispered. He got up, left the man dead in a pool of blood on the platform, and started to make his way out with the crowd when he bumped into a large man with a big stomach.

"Somebody has been killed, I'm getting upstairs to see what is going on," Father Reynolds said to Patrick Campbell.

The priest hurried up the stairway out to the street. Upon exiting the tunnel onto Michigan Avenue, he peered around the street corner and saw a frantic scene of people pouring out from the station. Father Reynolds was stunned to spot the light-haired accomplice standing on the corner.

The man appeared to be waiting for a pickup. Nobody stopped, so he ducked into a nearby store and asked to use the toilet. The suspect disappeared into the restroom, unwrapped a small piece of paper containing white powder, snorted the powder and left the paper behind in a stall for police to recover later. He walked hurriedly out of the store and disappeared down State Street.

Back inside the subway station, the dark-haired gunman had tossed the murder weapon on the cement and was now lost in a crowd of bedlam.

Father Reynolds had bolted from the scene without stopping to talk to police. He skipped his doctor's appointment and, instead, decided to get out of Chicago as quickly as possible and catch the next train back to South Bend.

By the time he returned to Notre Dame, news of the murder of Chicago Tribune reporter Jake Lingle had spread like a wildfire. Father Reynolds immediately tracked down his superiors at Notre Dame and told them what he witnessed.

Their collective order was direct: "Stay quiet... don't get involved."

The Lingle shooting - Chicago's 11th murder in 10 days – dominated headlines in the city and across the country. The Tribune editorialized that Lingle was killed because "... his killers either thought he was close to information dangerous to them or intended the murder as notice to the newspapers that crime was ruler in Chicago..."

Gangsters getting whacked in Chicago's most violent wave of gangland murders to date was everyday news. But the murder of this Chicago Tribune reporter initially appeared to be unprecedented – that is, until St. Louis Star reporter Harry T. Brundidge took it upon himself to investigate the case and shed light on the true story behind the Chicago crime reporter's murder.

Brundidge was one of the nation's premiere newspaper scribes, a superstar newshound who traveled to scenes of the biggest stories across the country and scooped the locals as prolifically as he ruled the presses in St. Louis. When it came to tapping underworld sources in Chicago to unravel the full story on the Lingle murder and shed light on the residual shock waves that reverberated through every newspaper that covered organized crime, Brundidge had no equal.

"Up here, where a gent is apt to get 'knocked off' for sending his shirt to the wrong laundry, a house of cards was built," Brundidge wrote in his piece on Lingle that appeared in the St. Louis Star two weeks after the murder on June 26, 1930. "Its foundation was beer, booze, graft, and all forms of racketeering and the architects were a lot of comic strip politicians, itchy-palmed coppers and some money-hungry newspapermen. They made a lotta promises and a lotta dough, and kept some of the former."

Brundidge keenly pointed out that Lingle was not the first newspaper reporter to get whacked after crossing the mob. Chicago Daily News tipster Julius Rosenheim was also gunned down for blackmailing bootleggers, gamblers and brothelkeepers, and threatening to expose criminal operations in the Daily News. And there were others, all of whom, like Rosenheim, may as well have died quietly behind the scenes from natural causes. Not until the hit on Jake Lingle had a newspaper reporter been gunned down in such a sensational public mob execution.

The news of Lingle getting rubbed out came as little surprise to the veteran newspaper reporter. Lingle's lavish lifestyle outside the Chicago Tribune - symbolized by the personalized diamond-studded belt buckle with the initials "A.J.L." gifted by Al Capone – had been common knowledge around Chicago's newsrooms, a fact spelled out succinctly during Brundidge's interview with Tribune publisher Col. Robert McCormick.

"I'm not asserting that Lingle was an honest man," McCormick said. "Neither am I denying that perhaps he was honest. But at the same time, I'll tell you he didn't have enough money to be as big a man in the underworld as he's said to have been, if the pay-off in that underworld is as big as it's supposed to be."

Reporters who mirrored Lingle's brazen style further fueled Brundidge's exploitation of a newspaper industry that had been compromised by the greed of more and more newspapermen who were doubling as mob accomplices.

Brundidge quickly flipped the switch on the initial false perception around Chicago that Lingle was killed because he had exposed the mob in unflattering crime stories. Calling the victim out as a reporter who profited handsomely by using his newspaper clout to work both sides of the law had stirred the suspicions of editors in newsrooms everywhere.

"(Lingle) wouldn't go to a ball game or a race track with anybody bearing a title lower than a deputy commissioner of police, and he became the only reporter in newspaper history who could bet $500 or $1,000 'across the board' on a horse race without having goose pimples while the ponies were running around the track," Brundidge wrote.

"Jake had paper profits in the stock market that made him think he was financially independent. Bright young men on other newspapers who emulated Jake's business methods moved out of little $90-a-month apartments and exchanged their Chevrolets for Cadillacs. The guy who didn't have a racket in Chicago was just a poor dumb wit. Jake… KNEW he had to be SEEN before a guy with any kind of a racket could make a move. Jake was giving $10 tips for two-bit service and spending a lot of time in Florida with 'Scarface' and other unnamed gents, and with these friends he also visited Cuban race tracks. His imitators among the newspaper fraternity were doing well, too. Some went to Europe on salaries that ordinarily wouldn't rate a vacation in an Ozark fishing camp.

"But…" Brundidge emphasized in his St. Louis Star column, "… all of this isn't telling readers of The Star why Jake Lingle was murdered or why a phone may ring at any moment now, bringing the news that another reporter got a ticket to the hot place where his 'past the fire lines' badge won't help him out a bit."

Police suspected the Aiellos, a crew of henchmen working for Bugs Moran on the North Side. Brundidge scoffed at the cops' shallow perception. Capone had called all the shots in Chicago since the St. Valentine's Day Massacre. If anybody knew who had shot Jake Lingle, it was Capone.

Brundidge set out to visit Capone at his Miami Beach estate, where he had been lying low since his release from prison a few months earlier in March. At 8:15 p.m. on July 17, Brundidge arrived unannounced, got off the train in Miami and checked in at the Pancoast Hotel in Miami. He hired a car service that drove him straight to Capone's plush estate on Palm Island. When he pulled up to the iron gates at the entranceway to the palatial residence, a guard said Capone was off somewhere with his attorney.

"When will he return?" Brundidge asked.

The guard shrugged. Brundidge took a seat on the ground and waited for Capone to return. At 10 p.m. sharp, a long limousine stopped in front of the gates. Brundidge noticed immediately that only Capone's younger brother was in the limo.

A few minutes later, a black sedan pulled up. The door opened. Capone himself stepped out flanked by two armed guards and another man.

Brundidge stuck out his hand and introduced himself. Capone recognized the reporter from the stories he had been reading in the papers about the Lingle murder.

"This is a surprise," Capone replied. "Come on in."

Brundidge had struck gold where no other newspaper man had dared to pan. He took a seat next to "Scarface Al" on a divan on the sun porch of Capone's magnificent home.

"You seemed to have raised merry hell in Chicago," Capone remarked. "What brings you here?"

Brundidge didn't mince words. "I thought I would ask you, who killed Lingle?"

"Why ask me?" Capone shot back. "The Chicago police know who killed him."

"Was Jake your friend?" Brundidge inquired.

"Yes, up to the day he died."

It was clear to Capone that Brundidge had done his homework. When Brundidge brought up rumors of "a row" between Capone and Lingle that had spread on the streets, Capone emphatically denied any riff by saying, "Absolutely not."

"It is said you fell out with him because he failed to split profits from handbooks," Brundidge pressed.

"Bunk," Capone snapped. "The handbook racket hasn't been really organized in Chicago for more than two years and anyone who says it is doesn't know Chicago."

The reporter noticed that Capone's tone grew shorter with each question. Capone appeared to be caught off guard when Brundidge asked if he had refused to see Lingle after his release from a correctional workhouse in Philadelphia.

"Who said I didn't see him?" Capone replied.

"The Chicago newspapers, the files of which, including his own paper, the 'Trib,' set forth the fact."

"Well," Capone responded, "if Jake failed to say I saw him, then I didn't see him."

Brundidge's inquisition shifted to the diamond-studded belt buckle Capone gave to Lingle as a gift. "Do you mind stating what it cost?"

"Two hundred fifty dollars," Capone said.

"Why did you give it to him?"

"He was my friend," Capone replied.

"How many rackets was he engaged in?" Brundidge quizzed.

Capone slightly bristled at the question with a shrug of his shoulders and a smirky grin. Brundidge sensed he was on the verge of getting more answers than this notorious gangster realized he would be giving up. The astute reporter dug in deeper.

"What was the matter with Lingle, the horse races?" Brundidge asked. "How many other Lingles are there in Chicago in the newspaper racket?"

"Phooey, don't ask," Capone hissed.

"Seriously," Brundidge pushed, "what do you think of newspaper men who turn their profession into a racket?"

"I think this," Capone replied in a circumspect tone. "Newspapers and newspaper men should be busy suppressing rackets and not supporting them. It does not become me, of all persons, to say that, but I believe it."

Brundidge saw his opening to go straight for the jugular. "How many newspaper men have you had on your payroll?"

Capone paused. Brundidge knew he had struck a sensitive nerve with the hardline question. Capone's black sociopathic eyes darkened even deeper as he submitted to an answer with a shrug.

"Plenty," Capone replied.

"Have you had any telephone calls from newspaper men in Chicago since publication in the St. Louis Star that Lingle was not the only one in his profession in Chicago with a racket?"

"Plenty," Capone repeated.

Capone leaned over. He put his arm around Brundidge's shoulders and squeezed a conciliatory squeeze that stirred up a bees' nest of anxiety in the reporter's stomach. Brundidge's line of questioning dug deep, perhaps too deep for Public Enemy No. 1's comfort zone. Capone answered every question, but Brundidge had toed a contentious line with the mob boss – a line that, if crossed, could result in the same tragic consequences for anybody who stuck their nose too deep into gangland business that had struck Jake Lingle.

"Listen, Harry, I like your face," Capone said. "Let me give you a hot tip. Lay off Chicago and the money hungry reporters. You're right... because you're right, you're wrong. You can't buck it, not even with the back of your newspaper, because it is too big a proposition. No one man will ever realize just how big it is, so lay off."

"You mean?" Brundidge pressed.

"I mean, they'll make a monkey out of you before you get through," Capone cautioned. "No matter what dope you have to give that grand jury, the boys will prove you're a liar and a faker. You'll get a trimming."

"I'm going to quote you as saying that," Brundidge declared.

Capone laughed off the mild admonishment. "If you do," he replied, "I'll deny it."

Tired of the questioning, Capone got up to show off his palatial property. They walked around the grounds surrounding Capone's villa, past the swimming pool and bath house, out to the private pier that facilitated a boat house, a high-powered speed boat and a lavish yacht.

"Let's quit talking about the rackets," Capone suggested as the two strolled under the moonlight along the waters of Biscayne Bay. "You've seen the grounds, now, how about a tour of my home?"

Brundidge followed Capone inside. By the time they had walked through all 17 rooms of the house – from the bedrooms to the kitchen where a nice catch of fresh mackerel was chilling on ice – it was 1 a.m.

Capone escorted Brundidge out to the front gate. After saying their goodbyes, one of Capone's men drove Brundidge back to his hotel. On the way back, the two struck up a conversation that lasted almost until the sun came up.

Back in Chicago, a mountain of press amplified daily with the investigation into who killed Lingle. Under "nine hundred million tons of pressure" from the public to resign, Lingle's pal, William Russell, stepped down from his post as police commissioner within a week of the murder.

"Someone had to be the red meat," Russell admitted. "I have had an insurmountable obstacle, by that I mean Prohibition, and I don't give a damn who knows it."

Also out was Chicago Police Deputy Commissioner John Stege, who had flaunted his rank to keep underlings from hassling bookmakers and gamblers who bought racing information from "Race Track Service" put out by the General News Bureau Inc. J.M. Regan, general manager of the General News Bureau, had been a close friend of Lingle's for years.

The Lingle murder had also exploded into a massive scandal for the Tribune. Chicago Mayor William Hale Thompson, a perennial target of the newspaper's scathing editorials, used the killing to go on the offensive by referring to the Tribune as the "Lingle Evangelistic Institute."

Frank Wilson, a federal agent for the Internal Revenue Service investigating Capone for tax evasion, wrote in his autobiography that Tribune owner Col. McCormick was well-aware of Lingle's gangland connections. The Colonel, according to Wilson, had even taken it upon himself to personally set up a meeting between Lingle and Wilson that was supposed to have taken place the day after the murder.

McCormick vehemently denied Wilson's accusations. Others close to the Tribune proprietor said Wilson only contacted McCormick after the murder.

The scandalous accusations lobbed toward the Tribune and the newspaper's brass overshadowed news reports that a priest had been spotted running from the scene. A police officer, and civilian Patrick Campbell, both claimed the priest was a "fake" who may have been involved in the murder. The police went public with widely circulated advertisements calling for the priest to come forward.

Father Reynolds was nervous and uncertain what to do. He prayed for spiritual guidance. When the priest met with his superiors at Notre Dame seeking advice, they gave him their blessing.

Father Reynolds was free to contact the authorities in Chicago and tell them what he had seen.

6

MOB STEPS

P olice hounded the streets of Chicago around the clock

to pin down a suspect. More than 1,000 criminals of record were hauled in for questioning while detectives narrowed the motive for the Lingle hit down to circumstances surrounding two competing dog tracks — the Hawthorne, owned by Capone, and the Fairview, controlled by Moran.

Street sources revealed a promise Lingle had made to help Moran put another track in operation on the West Side. Moran had paid Lingle $2,500 up front in return for using his clout to get The Stadium open without any interference from the law. But like so many times before, the promise of favor fell by the wayside with Lingle pocketing Moran's down payment.

The investigation was only a few hours old when the name of the hit's suspected orchestrator fell into detectives' laps. Police knew Jack "Jake" Zuta all too well.

Zuta operated several brothels on West Madison Street before going to work for Capone in the mid-1920s. He helped contribute $50,000 of Capone's money to Chicago Mayor William Hale Thompson's re-election campaign in 1927, but when the infamous gang war broke out between Capone and Moran, Zuta defected crosstown to Moran's North Side Gang.

Zuta was known as the crafty "brains" and vice ring director of the North Side Gang run by Moran and Giuseppe "Joe" Aiello, a bootlegger who for years perpetuated a relentless bloody feud with Capone. Aiello masterminded several failed attempts to kill Capone, and he fought former business partner and Capone ally Antonio Lombardo for control of the Chicago branch of the Unione Siciliana benevolent society.

Aiello and Moran both sanctioned the contract murder of Lombardo. Capone retaliated by ordering the St. Valentine's Day Massacre.

Moran's North Siders generally despised Zuta as a coward who would sacrifice his own mother to save himself under intense interrogation. They tolerated him because of his reputation for being a smart underworld businessman.

To Capone, Zuta was a traitorous pimp. A rat.

Police at first suspected Aiello and his crew. Acting on a tip, their suspicions shifted to Zuta, and they quickly moved to bring the Capone turncoat in for questioning.

Zuta was accompanied by a girl and two teenage members of the Moran gang when he was picked up by police on June 10, the day after the Lingle murder. The interrogation lasted nearly 24 hours.

It didn't matter that Zuta kept his mouth shut without incriminating anybody. Once word hit the streets that Zuta was talking to police, every wise guy in Chicago tagged the brothel keeper as a snitch to be taken out at the first opportunity. Nobody knew that Zuta's life was in danger of the same fate that befell Jake Lingle than Zuta himself.

"I'll be killed the minute I leave this building," Zuta told police the moment he was arrested. "Don't stand around looking sleepy. Do you cops want me killed? Here's the time I'll get it, if you're going to leave me to it. All of my people are hiding away. You cops have got to look out for me...

"My God," he pleaded, "I'm a goner. I know it."

Police got nothing from Zuta, and they told him to go home. He asked Lt. George Barker to drive him and his companions to the safety of his house on the North Side in Barker's own car, which was parked in the alley behind police headquarters.

Zuta and the three others piled into Barker's car. Zuta crouched on the floor in the rear to hide from street view. Barker slipped out of the alley successfully. A few minutes later the police lieutenant was driving toward Moran territory on the North Side where Zuta figured to be safe.

As Barker made a turn at Quincy and State streets, Zuta was on the floor jabbering in fear of his life. Barker no sooner edged the vehicle slowly into the traffic of the Loop when a blue Chrysler sedan swiftly drove up on them.

"They're after us!" Zuta screamed.

The sedan crashed squarely into Barker's car, causing it nearly to overturn. Barker drew his gun and started firing immediately at the sedan. The Chrysler swung around at full speed with guns blasting out all windows. A hailstorm of bullets turned the street into a thick, fiery fog.

A slew of police in separate squad cars rushed to the scene to try to pursue the blue sedan. But the gangsters' car sped away, miraculously avoiding several vehicles in the roadway and ignoring all signal lights in a high-speed escape westward.

By the time Barker had rushed back to his own vehicle, Zuta and his friends were gone. Smashed glass from store windows transformed State Street White Way into a crystal maze. Barker spotted a revolver in the middle of State Street which one of the killers had apparently tossed from the sedan. He picked it up and placed it in his car to take to Goddard Laboratories for ballistic tests.

A crowd had gathered around a nearby streetcar. The motorman, Elbert Lusader, lay dead after being shot with a stray bullet. In his final conscious act, Lusader had turned off the power of the crowded car. Another group surrounded Olaf Svenste, an employee of the Standard Club, who also caught a bullet in the crossfire and sat seriously wounded at the side of Barker's car.

Zuta had vanished. It was apparent to the State Attorney's office chief investigator, Patrick Roche, that Zuta's verbal fears prior to the attack and the verification of his despair in the shootout on State Street revealed, at the least, some knowledge as to who had pulled the trigger in the Lingle murder.

The following Saturday, Zuta failed to appear in court and his bail was forfeited.

"Needless to say, my client must protect himself," Zuta's attorney, Benjamin Cohen, explained to the judge. "He is certain of death if he appears in Chicago at this time. In view of recent developments, he can hardly expect adequate protection."

The gun Barker picked up off the street was tested at Goddard Laboratories. Ballistics results pointed to the South Side. The gun was revealed to have had the serial numbers filed off and covered with the symbol "#" - a Capone technique discovered previously on two guns used in a mob shooting that had been traced back to Capone crew members.

Rumors swirled that Zuta had fled Chicago and was hiding out in Kentucky. Zuta got out of Chicago all right, but he drove north to Wisconsin's Upper Nemahbin Lake, a few miles west of Milwaukee. He settled in at the Lakeview Hotel under the name "J.H. Goodman, of Aurora."

His cover identification was short lived.

On August 1, 1930, Zuta enjoyed himself in the dance pavilion adjoining the hotel. Twenty couples were dancing, and Zuta was the life of the party filling the mechanical piano with handfuls of nickels.

"Every time she stops, the nearest one will feed her a nickel," Zuta called out. "Let's go! This is the life!"

As Zuta made his announcement, three men walked up to the front entrance of the pavilion. They quietly picked up the doorman, Joe Selby, and carried him bodily to a nearby automobile. One of the men poked the doorman's ribs with a gun and sat next to him in the backseat. Selby counted eight well-dressed men who made their way to the outside corner of the pavilion.

Five went inside. One carried a machine gun.

Zuta was dancing. As he passed the door of the pavilion with his partner, five men grabbed Zuta by the shoulders. Zuta fell to the floor, his face white as paste. The men picked him up calmly without saying a word. They carried him to the piano, sat him down in a chair and flanked him. The man holding the machine gun stood about 10 feet away. Two others, both with guns drawn, herded the dancers to another corner away from the door.

Without as much as a glance toward the gunman toting the machine gun, Zuta sat stone-faced, rigid and silent. He started to fall from the chair when the men beside him stepped away.

The machine gun fired off a cavalcade of bullets that cut across the piano with a crash of glass and haphazard musical intensity. Zuta fell limp to the floor, dead on impact, his lifeless body riddled with 28 bullets.

"Don't come out of this place," the killer warned the rest of the dancers.

The hitmen abruptly exited the room and walked back to the getaway cars without the slightest attempt to hide their faces. Once the dancers realized the danger had subsided, men scurried to revive the unconscious women who had fainted.

A few weeks later, a barrel containing the remains of Pasqualino "Patsy" Tardi washed up in a shallow portion of

Lake Michigan. Rumors immediately surfaced that it was Tardi who had fumbled the gun and nearly botched the hit on Lingle. Those rumors died out quickly without any substantiation.

Amidst a slew of murders that gripped the city through newspaper headlines every day, Chicago police detectives continued to work under mounting pressure from the public to make an arrest in the Lingle hit. Every time police brought in a suspect for Father Reynolds to see, the priest would catch the South Shore and make the two-hour train trip from South Bend to get a look at a new face.

Some of the men brought in for Father Reynolds' eyes were small-time hoods being hassled out of mere police formality and otherwise had nothing to do with anything. Others were more notorious. Some were famously notorious.

"And, because I'd go in... I met all the best killers there, like Baby Face Nelson," Father Reynolds recalled. "He looked like a little dwarf, see, and then the most innocent face you ever saw, but the biggest killer in Chicago."

Chicago investigators didn't have a solid suspect. What they had was the weapon that had killed Lingle, a .38 caliber handgun dropped at the scene. The gun's serial number had been filed off, but ballistics expert Col. Calvin Goddard had a process for raising the tattoo – the second-deep impression left by the dye that stamped the serial number on a gun.

Within an hour of receiving the gun, Goddard traced the origin of Lingle's murder weapon to the Colt factory in

Hartford, Connecticut – the gun manufacturer that in June 1928 shipped the same .38 caliber and five similar revolvers to a sporting goods store on Diversey Parkway. The store's owner, Peter von Frantzius, was also known as the "Armorer" because of his reputation for being Chicago's most prolific arms dealer to the underworld.

While von Frantzius had committed no crime under the city's lax gun laws, a detective and accompanying Chicago Tribune reporter John Boettinger threatened to jam von Frantzius up in the public eye if he didn't cooperate. With no other options at hand, the gun dealer produced a sales receipt showing the gun was sold to Frankie Foster.

Police pushed von Frantzius for more information. The gun dealer also revealed that Foster had been accompanied by a man who insisted that von Frantzius file off the serial numbers on each of the guns. The man with Foster at the time of the gun purchase, Ted Newberry, had already been fingered by witnesses as one of the gunmen in the Lingle murder. But the mere accusation didn't hold enough water for investigators to make a case against Newberry.

Frankie Foster, on the other hand, was a solid suspect.

A short, stocky, dark-haired bootlegger of Romanian-Jewish heritage also known by the names Frank Frost, Frank Citro and Frank Bruna, Foster was a former member of Moran's North Side Gang who had defected to Capone's ranks with Ted Newberry. Two days after Lingle's murder, Foster fled to Los Angeles, where Capone and Moran were both rumored to be attempting to establish new operations on untapped West Coast turf.

The gun receipt provided Chicago authorities with ample legal ammunition to bring Foster back. He was indicted in absentia as an accessory before the fact to murder, picked up in Los Angeles, and extradited back to Chicago where Foster was held in Cook County Jail for four months.

Foster's lawyer's demands for trial went virtually ignored three times. By the time his attorney filed a motion for trial a fourth time, State Attorney John A. Swanson conceded that, despite the gun receipt in Foster's name, there was insufficient evidence to warrant any further prosecution. The case against Foster collapsed.

As the investigation moved forward, Tribune lawyer Charles F. Rathbun and Patrick T. Roche, chief investigator for the State's Attorney's office, began to sense that moves were being made on the South Side to mislead investigators to target Zuta as the orchestrator of the Lingle hit in an effort to put the focus of the investigation on Moran's North Side Gang. Since the St. Valentine's Day Massacre, Moran had been virtually powerless to order a hit as monumental as the Lingle killing.

Capone was at his palatial home in Miami lying low from the Lingle investigation brewing in Chicago and a federal Internal Revenue Service probe heating up over his income sources, yet, Rathbun and Roche knew he remained the undisputed boss of Chicago's underworld in the wake of the St. Valentine's Day Massacre. Capone might have been out of sight, but Chicago was still Capone's city. Capone continued to be the chief benefactor from any and all of the city's organized crime business.

Roche's suspicions that the Lingle hit stopped at Capone's South Side doorstep intensified when Zuta's ledger fell into his possession. The ledger was a last laugh from the grave that meticulously documented $400,000 in bank notes and canceled checks from men who either paid or owed Zuta money. Among the names listed included municipal court Judge Joseph Schulman; Judge Emmanuel Eller; Nate De Lue, assistant business manager of the Chicago Board of Education; Illinois State Senator Henry Starr, who claimed the $400 check he received from Zuta was for "legal services"; and former Illinois State Senator George Van Lent.

One letter from Zuta's records caught Roche's eye. One-time Capone bootlicker Louis La Carva had fallen out of favor with his former boss and had contacted Zuta to help exact revenge. "Dear Jack," the note read, "I'd help you organize a strong business organization capable of coping with theirs in Cicero."

Roche could barely contain his elation over Zuta's ledger. When a reporter asked if arrests were imminent in the Lingle investigation, he responded: "A lot of men will be leaving town… We are following the trail of many of Zuta's dollars, and there is no telling where it will end."

In September, the trail for Lingle's killer led Roche to Louisville, Kentucky, where Indiana gangster Ted Geisking had been tracked down on the loose tip that he may have been the "left-handed man" witnesses saw shoot Lingle.

But two witnesses failed to identify Geisking as the shooter. Both claimed to have seen a blond-haired gunman fleeing the scene. Geisking had dark hair. When Geisking passed the shampoo test given by Roche and proved he didn't dye his hair, the Indiana mobster was cleared of any link to Lingle's murder. He was returned to Indiana under police custody where he was wanted on numerous other charges.

In December, with the trail for Lingle's killer still lukewarm, Roche enlisted a former bank robber, beer runner and associate of the South Side Genna brothers' crew to return to his old gangland haunts as an undercover operative. It didn't take long for John Hagan to ingratiate himself with an old pal, Pat Hogan, who had been rumored to be vaguely connected with the Lingle murder.

Hagan took Hogan out night after night and plied him with food, drink and cabaret action in the hope that Hogan would spill something good. After several nights of carousing, a drunken Hogan blurted out a nickname.

"Buster."

Hagan played nonchalant toward Hogan's name-drop. Over the next few weeks Hagan continued to treat Hogan to a succession of nightclub-filled evenings while trying to casually pull more information about "Buster." Finally, during one night of particularly heavy drinking, Hogan divulged Buster's actual name, or at least the name Hogan knew.

"Leo Bader."

Hogan mentioned that Bader stayed at two apartments about a block away from each other: One at the Riviera Apartments at 4906 Blackstone Avenue; the other at the Lake Crest Drive Apartments at 4827 Lake Park Avenue.

When Roche learned that their suspect kept two addresses, the savvy sleuth knew he had a problem. It would be far too risky for investigators to move aggressively and make inquiries about Bader with staff members at either building. Roche was certain that if word got back to Bader that cops were asking questions around his residence, their main suspect would vanish in the wind.

One night after Roche had returned to his office from dinner with his captain, he sat in his chair with his feet perched on his desk puffing on a black cigar. Suddenly, it hit him: His former secretary at the Internal Revenue Service also lived on Lake Park Avenue.

"Sam…" Roche called to his captain, who was chatting with another investigator in the office. "Hand me that telephone book, will you? It seems to me I know a girl who worked for me in the federal building several years ago who lives near that number on Lake Park Avenue."

Roche took the book and shuffled through some pages. He stopped and ran his finger down a column to one name: Rose Huebsch.

For several years when Roche served as the ace of the IRS's Special Intelligence Unit, Rose Huebsch had worked as his secretary. It had been three years since he left the IRS to become chief investigator for State's Attorney Swanson, but Roche knew that Huebsch had stayed on with the IRS, and that she still worked at the Federal Building. She was 30 years old, barely 5 feet tall with a plump figure and dark hair, and possessed a quiet manner, but Roche remembered his former secretary as being keenly smart, exceptionally competent, and fearlessly confident.

He looked at the address listed next to her name in the phone book: 4827 Lake Park Avenue, the same address as Bader.

Roche picked up the phone and dialed Huebsch's number. She answered and expressed mild surprise at hearing from Roche. A brief conversation ensued before the two readily agreed to meet at his office in the Temple Building. Roche held off from giving Huebsch any details about the gangster they were seeking, nor did Huebsch ask. She was just glad to help her former boss.

Thirty minutes later, at about 8:30 p.m., Huebsch sat in Roche's office giving Roche and Rathbun a detailed description of the Lake Crest Drive apartment building —— a five-story structure considered modern for its time that facilitated 75 furnished apartments, mostly one-bedroom kitchenette-style units.

A quick check on Bader's name at the building revealed that the suspect did not have a private telephone in his apartment. Those who called were instructed to leave a message for Bader with the building's clerk. That bit of information gave Roche an idea: He asked Huebsch to return to her building, but instead of going straight to her apartment, she was instructed to check the building directory in the front entry corridor for Bader's name.

At 10 p.m., the phone rang in Roche's office. He picked up to Huebsch's excited voice on the other end. She had found Bader's name – and apartment number. Bader lived in Number 410, directly across a narrow, 6-foot-wide hallway from Huebsch's apartment in 411. Huebsch could open her front door and look straight into Bader's front door.

"Watch the door closely and let me know if you see or hear anything," Roche advised.

Ten minutes later, Roche's phone rang again. Huebsch's voice, again, was charged.

"I had my door standing open, and I sat beside a floor lamp reading a magazine," she said. "Then I heard the door of the elevator slam, and footsteps sounded in the hall. I looked up just in time to see a man pass and stop before Apartment 410. He pulled out his keys and entered."

"What did he look like?" Roche asked.

"Well, he was blond," Huebsch replied. "He looked like a bad man. He was fairly tall and well built."

Huebsch had only gotten a quick glance of the suspect, but the description matched perfectly with the man Roche and Rathbun were after. When Roche passed Huebsch's details on to another law enforcement investigator who confirmed the description, Roche and Rathbun both knew they had their man in their sights.

Rathbun and Roche also knew they had to move quickly if they were going to catch Bader on the spot. If the gangster got wind of their tail, he could disappear in a flash. And if news hit the streets that the heat was on Bader at his address, his associates would spread the word and the entire investigation could be jeopardized.

On December 21, Rathbun, Roche, fellow investigators Fred Joyner, Walter Wendt and Samuel Lederer, and Tribune reporter John Boettinger, walked through a heavy snow fall to the Lake Crest Drive Apartments and set up posts in the front and rear of the building. Two men were also posted in the shadows beneath Bader's window in case he discovered the sting and tried to escape down a rope. A third man walked slowly up and down the sidewalk as cars, street cars and taxi cabs passed. His eye never left the front doorway of the apartment building.

Inside Huebsch's apartment, Roche gave her the signal to dial the number of the apartment building and ask the clerk to call Bader. The plan was for Huebsch to tell the operator to ring Bader's buzzer to say there was a message left for him at the front desk. Hopefully, Bader would leave his apartment so the investigators could move in and capture him.

But it was past 11 p.m. – the plan hit a snag.

"We called the apartment building office," Huebsch told Roche after hanging up the phone. "They told me that the call service was discontinued at 11 o'clock at night, and that they would be unable to call Mr. Bader to the telephone. I asked the girl to ring his buzzer, but she said she couldn't do it."

With snow falling heavily outside and Bader seemingly settled in his apartment for the night, there was no further need for guards posted at the front and rear of the building. The men outside had grown impatient, so they climbed a back stairway and quietly made their way up to Huebsch's apartment on the fourth floor. With the door cracked open a mere two-to-three inches to serve up a full view of Bader's apartment door, the investigators took turns throughout the night posted in Huebsch's kitchenette with an eye out for any movement coming through the front door of the apartment across the hall.

The sun came up following the all-night stakeout. Roche decided once again to have Huebsch call the front desk and leave a message for her neighbor. Huebsch dialed the phone from her own apartment. She told the operator to contact Bader with a message that a call from a woman was waiting for him at the building's office.

All eyes were on the front door across the hall when it opened. A tall, powerfully-built man with light hair emerged partially dressed from the apartment and made his way down the hallway. Before the occupant known as Leo Bader could get to the elevator, Roche, Rathbun and the rest of the stakeout crew converged on Chicago's most wanted murder suspect and arrested him without a fight.

The lady who lured Leo V. Brothers into a trap had no idea whom she had just helped her former boss capture.

"There isn't anything to tell about it," Huebsch told reporters who tracked her down at her office in the Federal Building later that day. "When Mr. Roche was in the federal service, I was his secretary. I was glad to help him… I used to transcribe reports in criminal cases, but this is the first one I've had anything to do with."

Leo Bader's real name was Leo Brothers, a Capone crew member who went by several aliases. Brothers had started out as a small-timer with the Egan's Rats crew, a ruthless organized crime gang that exerted considerable power in St. Louis for nearly 35 years. Brothers had worked his way up in the Egan's Rats organization as a labor-union buster and contract murderer specializing in arson, bombs and explosives. In 1929, while under indictment for murder in St. Louis, Brothers had fled to Chicago where he quickly found work with Capone.

Brothers was booked, charged with Lingle's murder, then whisked away to a secluded spot in the custody of the state's attorney's office. Rathbun and Roche both made it clear in no uncertain terms that it was mandatory for the continuing investigation to remain secret or else apprehension of other men suspected in the plot could be jeopardized.

Other than a handful witnesses who told police they saw a "blond man" running away from the train station after Lingle was shot, there was no solid evidence to identify Brothers as the gunman. With a receipt for the actual murder weapon in hand, there was more evidence connecting the Lingle murder with the man police had just released, Frankie Foster.

Nevertheless, Leo V. Brothers, a.k.a. Leo V. Bader, or "Buster," was Roche's guy.

Father Reynolds knew better.

After numerous trips to Chicago to view a seemingly endless slew of photo lineups, Father Reynolds remained certain that Frankie Foster was the man who had shot Jake Lingle. Even the one other direct eyewitness to the shooting, a woman standing with her husband when the killing went down, agreed with Father Reynolds. She, too, had viewed a wide array of photos. She told the priest she was also certain Foster acted as the shooter.

"And it shocked her so much, she went out for a glass of water in order not to faint, and when she came back the police had removed the picture," Father Reynolds said.

Father Reynolds was suddenly caught between the rock of God's truth and a dubious indictment. It was obvious to the priest that Chicago's law-enforcement crew was manufacturing a sure-fire conviction to answer for a high-profile murder. Foster was free and Brothers was in custody to answer for Lingle. To appease the public and justify another unsolved homicide, they would sell Brothers as Lingle's killer to a highly charged public starved for a conviction.

The Tribune congratulated Rathbun and Roche - and patted itself on the back for orchestrating the Brothers' arrest. The city's other newspapers remained just as skeptical in doubting Brothers' guilt as Father Reynolds. Editorials insinuated that Brothers was either the innocent victim of a frame-up, or he had allowed himself to be framed for money.

Word got out that Capone had handed up Brothers to the state as a sacrificial lamb. Capone, already the prime target of a heavy examination by the IRS, didn't want his name tied to any illegal business operations that could be exposed during the course of a federal trial. Two men with explicit knowledge of Capone's illegal financial sources – Lingle and Zuta — were both dead, and all the incessant raids and arrests of suspected gangsters conducted by police on Rathbun's and Roche's orders had come to an end.

Brothers' capture gave police, prosecutors and the local press what the public demanded — a gangster to convict, a blond gangster no less, like the one spotted at the scene. Most importantly to Capone, Brothers had no knowledge whatsoever of the notorious gangland boss's finances.

The fall guy did not come without a price. Capone was rumored to have promised Brothers a substantial payout for his time and trouble. Whispers on the street also implied that Capone was greasing the palms of police friends and his crooked pals in Chicago's judicial system to leave Foster alone. Capone would need Foster to counter Moran if a new turf war between the two Chicago mob bosses broke out on the West Coast.

Patrick Campbell, the bystander Father Reynolds had bumped into on the way out of the station, was alleviated of any obligation to serve as a witness by prosecutors. The woman, her husband, and Father Reynolds were set to be among the prosecution's eight key witnesses against Leo V. Brothers — that is, until the woman's nerves got the better of her and she begged her way off the witness stand.

Six witnesses were set to testify they saw Brothers fleeing from the Michigan Avenue tunnel; not one of whom could positively identify Brothers as the gunman. Lead prosecutor C. Wayland Brooks let Father Reynolds know in no uncertain terms whom they wanted him to point out as Lingle's murderer: It wasn't Frankie Foster.

"I want you to say this boy that we picked up is the one you saw running away up the alley," Brooks told the priest.

"No," Father Reynolds replied. "I won't do that because he doesn't correspond. If I was casting a play and I wanted a character representing the blond boy, I would pick him if I couldn't get any other better representative."

"No, it's alright," the prosecutor urged. "We want you to."

"He has a kind of faint resemblance," Father Reynolds noted reluctantly.

"Then we can't use you," the prosecutor countered.

"That's just fine," the priest said. "I have a lot of work to do back at Notre Dame and I'll catch a train back."

"Oh, no," Brooks retroceded with a laugh. "We can use you."

7

IN THE EYES OF
CAPONE

Father Reynolds returned to South Bend to await the

trial.

Prosecutors were content to let Father Reynolds go about his business at Notre Dame. They put their trust in the priest to show up on Friday, March 27th, 1931, the day he would take the witness stand and help them convict Leo Brothers in the shooting death of Jake Lingle.

Word got out that Father Reynolds had already identified Frankie Foster as the shooter. Investigators had Foster's name on the murder weapon's receipt, which only confirmed what had leaked out to the streets: Father Reynolds had already fingered Foster in a photo lineup as the dark-haired assailant who had snatched the gun away from the fumbling blond accomplice and fired a bullet into

Lingle's head. On the word of a priest under oath in front of Brothers' jury, the charges could shift to Foster, and Capone could lose one of his most valuable cogs in his plan to move West and challenge Moran for control of new turf that was being established in Los Angeles.

Whacking a double-crosser like Lingle or a rat like Zuta was mob business as usual. But to kill a priest? That was against the rules for even the most ruthless of criminals. Consequences would rain down in a holy hailstorm from all directions of the law, the press, the public, and rival gangsters who regularly sought out the blessings of the Catholic religion, not to mention the powerful institution that served as Father Reynolds' employer – Notre Dame.

Capone's men had orders to scare Father Reynolds into staying home, far away from the witness stand. Already the target of a massive IRS probe into his finances, Capone couldn't afford the blood of a Catholic priest on his hands, too. Persuading Father Reynolds to stay in South Bend and shun the witness stand in Chicago was another matter.

Capone's bootlegging business stretched from Chicago to Canada back to his hometown of New York City, so he was no stranger to Michigan. He owned at least one home in his name in the Upper Peninsula city of Escanaba. For privacy purposes Capone kept several hideout residences in associates' names, two of which were located just north of South Bend in the towns of Paw Paw and Berrien Springs.

*Capone was a frequent visitor to South Bend. One favorite haunt, Martha's Midway Tavern & Dance Hall, was a small watering hole tucked on 4th Street in a predominantly Belgian neighborhood in the neighboring town of Mishawaka.

Once, upon sampling Martha's special batch of homemade corn liquor the tavern owner conjured up in her back yard, Capone offered a business opportunity.

"Let me sell your liquor in Chicago and you could make a lot of money," Capone suggested.

Martha declined politely. "I only make it for the neighbors," she replied. "I want to keep it small. It's just for my neighbors."

Later, when Martha relayed Capone's offer to her husband, she admitted the blunt truth for her refusal. "There's no way I'm going to do business with that man," Martha insisted.

Sending iniquitous men out to lurk in the shadows to follow Father Reynolds in an attempt to intimidate him into not testifying at the Brothers' trial proved an easy logistical mode of operation for Capone. Father Reynolds was an extremely intelligent man with an acute sense of his surroundings that some would describe as "street sense." Once he committed to help police identify Lingle's killer, Father Reynolds firmly grasped the stark reality that he couldn't step foot out of his residential quarters at Morrissey Hall without watching his back.

The priest also suspected that if something were to happen to him, it wouldn't happen anywhere near the scene of the crime in Chicago. "Chicago is all Catholic," Father Reynolds reasoned.

But Chicago hardly provided sanctuary for the potential witness in the city's most high-profile murder trial. In one incident, the wife of an acquaintance met Father Reynolds on the street and invited him up to their apartment for a drink.

"That smelt high of murder," Father Reynolds declared. "I knew if I didn't take it, that would offend them, and if I did take it, I would be under a certain obligation, see, to them."

Never one to back down from a drink under any circumstance, Father Reynolds took the whiskey. "Of the two evils I chose the lesser one by taking the pint of whiskey and still living. You have to make a decision like that on an occasion like that."

Thanksgiving Day, 1930, Father Reynolds had just finished saying mass for students at Morrissey Hall. Leaving everybody in the dining room, Father Reynolds walked outside alone, where he was approached by a man dressed in a long coat. The suspicious man took a picture of Jake Lingle out of one pocket, then pulled a photo of Leo Brothers out of his other pocket.

"Are you going to testify against this man?" he asked.

"Well," Father Reynolds replied, "my lawyer told me that if anybody asked a question like that, I was to tell them that they must see my lawyer."

The priest's brazen retort caught the man by surprise. He turned and disappeared back into the shadows.

During trips to Chicago to view photo lineups, Father Reynolds left the police station and headed to temporary quarters that appeared to be set up for him at the German House Hotel. The German House served as a smoke screen. Every night after he had checked in to the German House, a police officer arrived in a car to pick up Father Reynolds at the German House and take him to the Polish Catholic parish on the North Side, zooming in and out of traffic through the Loop with a police signal.

Capone's street soldiers still seemed to know when the prosecution's star witness was in town. One afternoon, while waiting to catch the train at the Harrison Street station, Father Reynolds was startled to see a car pull up next to the station. A familiar face climbed out, followed by six intimidating goons who lined up behind Father Reynolds. One pulled a gun from his side pocket and shifted it inside his coat in full view of the priest.

"And this fellow kept looking at me," Father Reynolds recalled. "And I kept looking at him. And they knew that I knew that he was the killer, see."

Frankie Foster stood face-to-face with Father Reynolds. The priest, being the tough kid who grew up handing out his share of beatings in Bellows Falls, stood his ground. He remained outwardly calm, reserved, yet keenly aware of the immediate surroundings, trying to calculate a defense with one eye on a nearby metal chair.

"Well," he said, "I looked at the back of the chair and I was wondering whether that would stop a bullet or not because I was going to duck if they started firing. But I knew I had two things going for me, two strikes on them. One, I was a priest. Secondly, I was Irish, and if he killed an Irish priest in Chicago, the whole city would turn against him."

Seeing a strength in the priest he hadn't fully prepared for, Foster instantly packed it in without as much as a nod.

"Come on," he said to his goons. Foster turned around and returned to the car with all six men following close behind.

"Like little children, see," Father Reynolds recalled. "And I breathed easily, see?"

The intimidation tactics didn't stop at shady characters following the priest from the streets of Chicago to the campus of Notre Dame. Two anonymous letters addressed to Father Reynolds arrived at Morrissey Hall on two separate occasions. Both carried the same ominous message:

"Notre Dame will be more sorry than it realizes if they allow you to testify."

Father Reynolds gave a passing thought to turning the letters over to his superiors at Notre Dame. Then he tossed them in a waste basket.

8

A TICKET

Knute Rockne was a champion again.

Rockne's Ramblers brought an end to their 1930 season with a stunning thrashing of archrival USC, 27-0, a good old-fashioned Fighting Irish butt-whooping in front of a massive crowd of 90,000 at the Los Angeles Coliseum that sealed Rockne's third undefeated and untied national championship in 13 years as head coach of Notre Dame.

The star of that title-winning domination served as testimony to Rockne's untethered prowess as a leader and motivator of young men. Of all the legendary players to take the field for the Fighting Irish under Rockne's command – George Gipp, Dutch Bergman, Adam Walsh, the Four Horsemen – it was third-string running back Paul "Bucky" O'Connor from Bellows Falls, Vermont, who carried the load for the Irish on Dec. 7, 1930, rushing for 142 yards on 11 carries and scoring a touchdown.

In the season's immediate aftermath, Rockne helped organize a charity game in New York against the New York Giants to raise money for the city's food lines overwhelmed by unemployed New Yorkers victimized by the Great Depression. Rockne made a promise to O'Connor: "Play in the charity game, and I'll help you get into medical school at Yale University at no expense to your family." It was a promise Rockne kept.

Rockne was the undisputed king of the college football world. His fabled career record stood at 105-12-5, a mind-boggling winning percentage of .881. Once the trophies were handed out and the offseason was underway at the outset of 1931, Rockne was a hot commodity. Chronic health issues exacerbated by severe exhaustion plagued the coach, but he stubbornly planned to embark on a strenuous nationwide tour giving speeches to salesmen working for the Studebaker Corporation, the South Bend-based automobile manufacturer that provided Rockne with a very lucrative side income as a promotion manager. Already in the planning stages was Studebaker's next model, the "Rockne."

Flying was the only way for Rockne to travel around the country and meet the time demands of his grueling schedule.

"What's the use of wasting time on trains and automobiles?" he quipped to a friend. "This is a fast day and age. I've got to get around to do things and reach places."

Rockne's first offseason priority was to catch his breath with some rest and relaxation in Florida with his wife,

Bonnie, their daughter, Mary Jeanne, 10, their youngest boy Jackie, 4, and their oldest sons, Bill, 15, and Knute Jr., 12, both of whom were on spring break from their boarding school at Kansas City's Pembroke Hill.

Two years of suffering with phlebitis that landed Rockne in a wheelchair for an extended period of time during the previous football season had not subsided. Doctors constantly warned him that the relentless stress of coaching football at a national championship level on top of a grueling personal business calendar was taking a severe toll on his soon-to-be 43-year-old body.

Traveling to Florida, Rockne caught a plane out of Chicago with stops in Atlanta and Jacksonville, then it was on to Miami. When the plane was in the air, Rockne turned to fellow passenger L.W. "Chip" Robert, a trustee at Georgia Tech and friend of the coach, and remarked: "I think that each of us has a time to go, and when that time comes, no matter where we are, it strikes. So, I figure I might as well be in a plane as anywhere else."

The Rocknes vacationed at their winter home in Coral Gables. On Saturday, March 21, Rockne and Bonnie hooked up with friends, Frank and Mary Wallace, for a relaxing evening at Hialeah Race Track. Afterwards, he told a writer the vacation was agreeing with him, he was feeling much better, and he was looking forward to the upcoming football season. He also found time to kick around a football in the front yard with his young son, Jackie.

With the opening of spring football practice set to begin at Notre Dame, Rockne left Bonnie and his four children in Coral Gables, hopped a plane and returned to South Bend to preside over the team's first spring drills.

Two days into the sessions, Rockne fielded a phone call from his agent, Christy Walsh. There was a $50,000 offer on the table to come to Hollywood to work as an adviser on the planned Universal Pictures film project, "The Spirit of Notre Dame."

Walsh added that the Hollywood filmmakers wanted Rockne in California the following week to sign a contract. In addition to movie business, the two-day trip was crammed with personal appearances: Rockne was set to be inducted into the L.A. Breakfast Club, and he would be the featured speaker at a convention for Studebaker executives to promote the soon-to-be-named "Rockne" Studebaker car. Chicago pal John H. Happer, comptroller for Great Western Sporting Goods, also wanted Rockne to help open a new Great Western store in Los Angeles.

Flying to the West Coast was the only way Rockne could meet all his Los Angeles business obligations in two days. He could also return to Kansas City on April 12 to speak at Pembroke Hill's athletics banquet, the military school sons Bill and Knute Jr. attended.

It didn't take long for Rockne to realize that he needed a plane reservation, but a ticket was difficult to find at the last minute. Faced with the need for a plane ticket to Los Angeles with no other alternative except for a long time-consuming train trip, Rockne's only recourse at the moment was to let Christy Walsh handle ticket arrangements.

Rockne had other pressing concerns. Spring football practice was his top priority.

Father Reynolds was anxious to get the Brothers' trial over with and behind him. Badly in need of some rest and relaxation far away from the threat of mobsters following him from Chicago to South Bend, far away from the pressures his Notre Dame superiors had been applying to get him out of this trial and avoid the school's name being splashed all over the headlines of one of the most notorious gangland murders in recent memory, the priest had already secured a plane ticket to the West Coast where he planned to get away by enjoying his favorite hobby: hiking in the forests of Oregon.

Those plans were in jeopardy. Father Reynolds was the prosecutors' main witness. He had to make himself readily available at a moment's notice until the trial was completed. And he had to teach his American History class at Notre Dame the following week when students returned from spring break.

On Thursday, March 26, the night before he was scheduled to take the stand, Father Reynolds caught the South Shore train in South Bend and headed to Chicago. It was the usual routine of the past nine months: Check in at the German House, then slip out secretly under the protection of a police officer who drove Father Reynolds to the North Side to bed down at the local parish.

The trial was nearing the end of its second week. Eight witnesses called by prosecutor Curly Brooks described Lingle's killer as a man nearly 6-feet tall, well-built, young "like a college senior," wearing a gray suit and straw skimmer over light brown or blond hair. The blond man, according to the witnesses, was seen walking quickly toward Lingle moments before the fatal shot was fired in the tunnel, then doubling back the way he had come and dashing out of the tunnel after the shooting.

Six witnesses had pointed to Leo Brothers sitting at the defendant's table and identified him as the man who shot Jake Lingle. Seven witnesses testified to not seeing Brothers at the scene.

Before Father Reynolds took the witness stand on Friday, March 27, a photographer shot a photograph of the priest sitting in a chair in a waiting room down the hall from the courtroom. Seeing the camera, he tried to hide his nerves but the lens captured a frightened look that could not conceal the truth: Father Reynolds' eyes were filled with the fear of God.

That fear subsided on the witness stand. With Leo Brothers sitting at the defendant's table next to his attorney, Louis Piquett – the same Louis Piquett who had met with Lingle the night before Lingle was shot to death, and the same defense attorney who would later gain national prominence defending John Dillinger – Brooks fired off a series of questions before asking Father Reynolds to look Brothers in the eye and identify him as the gunman who shot Jake Lingle.

"He answered the description," Father Reynolds replied obtusely.

It's the most accurate account Father Reynolds could muster without defying his Bible-sworn oath, but hardly the rock-solid ID the prosecutor sought from the priest in front of the jury.

For months, those random threatening confrontations and anonymous letters had made it perfectly clear that the underworld didn't want Father Reynolds to testify. His civil duty was finally completed. Father Reynolds got off the witness stand, walked out of the courtroom, and left the courthouse with the sole intention of catching the next train back to South Bend and putting the entire ordeal behind him.

The next day, Father Reynolds unwound with a peaceful Saturday afternoon stroll on campus. Walking in front of the main building, the Golden Dome, he spotted a familiar face approaching from the opposite side of the courtyard.

Father Reynolds recognized his pal Knute Rockne immediately. The two had been friends since 1916 when Rockne was Notre Dame's track coach, and Father Reynolds was a star of the track team who had set a national record for the 2-mile run.

They greeted each other with open arms. After a brief chat about the trial, Rockne mentioned the Universal Pictures offer. The filmmakers wanted him to travel to Hollywood the following week to lend his expertise during production of "The Spirit of Notre Dame," a film starring Lew Ayres and Andy Devine.

There had been other film offers the past few years, but each one focused on Notre Dame football, and each was met with opposition from the Notre Dame hierarchy who wanted to distance themselves from football in favor of portraying the school as an academic institution. This offer was different. Rockne told Father Reynolds how excited he was to get out to Hollywood and finalize his contract to work on this movie. There was a jam-packed two-day schedule planned the minute he arrived. However, it was difficult to find a plane ticket to Los Angeles in such a short time, and a train would take too long to get to the West Coast.

Father Reynolds looked Rockne in the eye. He pulled out the flight reservation to the West Coast that he was unable to use.

"Take it, Rock," Father Reynolds said. "I'm in no hurry to get to Los Angeles."

The ticket was for Transcontinental & Western Flight 599, a passenger/postal delivery flight set to leave Kansas City for Los Angeles on Tuesday, March 31.

It was a perfect flight to accommodate Rockne's tight two-day West Coast schedule: He could travel to Chicago on Sunday, take the overnight train to Kansas City Monday night, and arrive just in time Tuesday morning to have a brief rendezvous with his sons, Bill and Knute Jr. The boys were still with their mother in Florida for the family's spring vacation trip, and they were expected to return by train to Kansas City at 8 a.m. on March 31. The timing was tight, but it did allow Rockne a few precious minutes with his sons before the plane departed Kansas City at 8:30 a.m.

This flight put Rockne in Los Angeles by nightfall – where his two close friends, "Navy Bill" Ingram, head coach of California, and his old pal, Pop Warner, who had moved on to coach Stanford, had already flown from San Francisco and were awaiting a reunion.

Rockne stuck out his hand and thanked the priest for the ticket. Father Reynolds grasped his pal's hand without mentioning anything about the mob intimidation tactics that had followed him the past few months.

The trial was over for Father Reynolds. Two anonymous letters he received on two separate occasions at his residence at Morrissey Hall, the last of which arrived in his mail just a few days before he took the witness stand, were in the trash and all but forgotten. "Notre Dame will be more sorry than it realizes if they allow you to testify" was a message that was gone with the wind.

Rockne was grateful for the priest's generosity. The two said goodbye and went their separate ways.

Section 2: The Crash

9

DELAYED FLIGHT

"I know if I hadn't given Rock my tickets, he would have been alive."

Father John Reynolds

Using the plane ticket purchased in Chicago by Father Reynolds, Christy Walsh handled the transfer of reservations for the flight leaving Kansas City on Tuesday into Rockne's name.

Before catching the train in South Bend and heading to Chicago on Palm Sunday evening, Rockne drove from his home on East Wayne Street and stopped in to visit his former neighbors, Tom and Kate Hickey, at their home on East St. Vincent Street a few blocks away from the Notre Dame campus.

After living next door to each other on St. Vincent Street for six years, the Hickeys and the Rocknes had become close friends. Tom Hickey accompanied Rockne on several road trips, and the two often shared sleeping compartments during those trips. Hickey had even served as Rockne's godfather during Rockne's baptism in Notre Dame's Log Chapel on November 20, 1925, when Rockne converted to Catholicism.

The Hickeys had a driveway to park cars, but Rockne, as was his custom, parked on the street and walked up the stairs to the front door. It was a nice visit. Rockne was his usual jovial self, down on the floor playing football with the Hickeys' 3-year-old son, Joe.

Toward the end of his stay, Rockne positioned himself by the home's front entryway and hiked the ball to the toddler. The ball sailed over the boy's head and smashed Kate Hickey's favorite Chinese vase.

Rockne shrugged his shoulders, smiled an apologetic grin, then told his friends goodbye and Tom Hickey watched his pal saunter down the walkway to his car and drive off.

*Rockne caught the South Shore train in South Bend headed to Chicago. Upon arrival, he went straight to his mother's house. Martha Gjermo Rockne's 72nd birthday was filled with cake and champagne.

On Monday, Rockne stopped in at the Chicago Herald-Examiner for a conversation with the paper's sports editor, Warren Brown. That evening before catching the train to Kansas City, he met up with Christy Walsh and Chicago playwright Albert C. Fuller over dinner and cigars.

"Soft landings, Coach," Fuller said in farewell as Rockne hopped into a cab.

"Yes," Rockne replied. "But, you mean, happy landings."

The cab dropped Rockne off at the train station in time to catch the overnight train to Kansas City that departed Chicago just before midnight.

Rockne rode the train through the night. When he arrived in Kansas City at about 7 a.m. the next morning, his pal and former Notre Dame teammate on the 1912 and 1913 squads, Dr. Dominic Michael "D.M." Nigro, greeted him at Union Station. The two longtime friends had breakfast in the Union Station dining room while they waited for the train carrying Bill and Knute Jr. to arrive from Florida.

But the boys' train was late. Rockne's flight was scheduled to depart Kansas City Municipal Airport at 8:30 a.m., he didn't have time to wait. Figuring to see his boys when he returned April 12 to speak at the Pembroke Hill athletic banquet, Rockne and Dr. Nigro took off for the airport to catch the T&WA flight in time.

After arriving at Kansas City Municipal Airport, Rockne took a few minutes to wire a telegram to Bonnie, who was still on vacation at their home in Coral Gables.

Rockne's friend, John Happer, was also ready to board the flight to Los Angeles. Rockne planned to help Happer set up a new Great Western Sporting Goods store in Los Angeles. The other passengers on the 10-seat airliner included C.A. Robrecht, a produce businessman from Wheeling, West Virginia; Waldo B. Miller, of Hartford,

Connecticut, an assistant superintendent of sales promotion in the group life and disability department of Aetna Insurance company; Spencer Goldthwaite, a young New Yorker traveling to Pasadena to visit his parents; and H.J. Christen, of Chicago.

Christen, who worked as a dime store interior designer in Chicago, was traveling to California in an effort to reconcile with his estranged wife. Just before leaving Chicago, Christen had cashed a check for $55,000, a massive sum of money for a storeroom designer to be carrying in 1931. The Chicago Tribune, the Chicago Herald-Examiner and the Chicago Evening Post had just paid out a combined $55,000 in reward money to the unknown informant responsible for the arrest and conviction of Leo Brothers, the Capone hitman on trial for killing Chicago Tribune reporter Jake Lingle.

But there was a problem. Passengers were notified that T&WA Flight 599 had been held up to wait for a late mail shipment due to arrive at any time. Jack Frye, TWA's vice president of operations, pushed the flight's takeoff time back to 9:15 a.m.

Rockne was anxious to get to Los Angeles. Frye's refusal to order the pilot, Capt. Robert (Joe-Pete) Fry, to put the plane in the air on schedule did not sit well with the fiery football coach. In full view of T&WA station operations department worker Wes Bunker, Rockne cornered Captain Fry and exerted some of his infamous motivation on the experienced former military fighter pilot.

"I paid for the ticket and you're paid to fly, let's go!" Rockne insisted loudly enough for everyone within earshot to hear. Fry stared at the ground. He shuffled his feet. A few seconds later, the pilot shrugged his acknowledgement.

Finally, the mail shipment arrived. Four seats on the plane were removed to make room for additional mail pouches that carried nearly 95 pounds of weight.

The passengers boarded the plane. Rockne was the last passenger to settle into a wicker chair with a leather cushion and no seatbelt. At about 9:45 a.m., Transcontinental & Western Flight 599 – a Fokker F-10 Trimotor, three-engine monoplane made out of laminated wood – was in the air.

Bad weather with rain, thick clouds and poor visibility between Kansas City and the first scheduled stop in Wichita prompted Fry and co-pilot Jess Mathias to navigate the first leg of the flight under low-hanging clouds. With reports of clear skies ahead, both pilots switched back and forth on the radio checking weather conditions with air traffic controllers at Wichita airport.

Rockne and the passengers were oblivious to the activity in the cockpit. Rockne peered out the window, but it was too cloudy for visibility. He felt the plane shake under his seat with turbulence. Numerous cross-country flights had made Rockne an experienced air traveler. He didn't think twice about the mild turbulence under his seat.

A radar map tracking the flight in Wichita indicated suddenly that the plane was altering its direction. Wichita flight controllers speculated a possible return to Kansas City. At exactly 10:45 a.m., a terse radio transmission from Mathias sent a chill through their airwaves.

"No time to talk," the co-pilot said.

Radio communication went dead.

Ranchers R.Z. Blackburn, Edward Baker and Clarence H. McCracken were working their daily farm chores on the ground when they spotted a large wooden aircraft flying at only about 600 feet. Young Edward Baker looked up from feeding cattle and recognized the plane as the mail airliner that frequently flew over his father's farm.

What Edward Baker witnessed next was something out of a bad dream: "A terrific explosion in the foggy sky..." is how a newspaperman would describe Baker's eyewitness account later that day in the March 31, 1931, evening edition of the Sedalia (Mo.) Democrat. "Looking up, the youth saw an airplane burst into flames and rocket toward the earth..."

One of the Fokker Trimotor's wings ripped away and fluttered to the ground like a giant piece of paper. The plane spiraled out of the cloudy sky and crashed into a wheat field owned by Edward Baker's father, Steward H. Baker, near the tiny community of Bazaar, Kansas.

The impact was violent, loud and ground-shaking.

"The plane was flying low and seemed to explode in the air," Edward Baker's mother told a reporter. "My son watched it spin in flames and bury itself in the soft pasture."

After shelling corn with his parents and brothers in their kitchen, 13-year-old Easter Heathman headed out to the barn on an errand when he heard a raspy, coughing roar that sounded like cars racing on the highway about a mile away. A phone call from a neighbor informed the Heathman family that a plane had crashed nearby at 10:37

a.m. The Heathmans jumped in their Model T and were among the first to arrive at the scene.

"My Uncle Clarence seen it come out of the clouds," Easter Heathman recalled. "He said the wing was broke off. The plane was turning end-over-end. You can picture in your own mind what that ride was like.

"There was the smell of gasoline and hot oil," Heathman noted.

The crash scene was catastrophic. Pieces of airliner furnishings, wood and debris scattered through the air for hundreds of feet. The impact was so tremendous, the tail of the plane was twisted and broken, resting at right angles to what was left of the fuselage – a fuselage made of solid steel tubing, bent, twisted and broken far beyond salvageable reclamation.

Edward Baker walked up on five bodies lying in a line about 30 feet from the tail near a long pile of broken wood, torn fabric and pieces of the aircraft, all reeking of gasoline and hot oil. The bodies of both pilots and John Happer were still in the plane's nose cone.

Another body came to rest on the ground near the wreckage. The left hand of the unrecognizable remains of Knute Rockne clutched a rosary.

Stunned responders had no idea who the victims were; no clue that the mangled body pulled out of the wreckage by three teams of horses — with his spinal column split wide open, his head mutilated beyond recognition, and his right arm driven into the pit of his stomach — belonged to the most famous football coach in the land, beloved by fans all over the world.

The Heathmans remained at the site until the coroner arrived about an hour later. Easter and his family helped carry bodies on stretchers to the ambulances that transported them to Kansas City. They also helped pick up scattered mail around the site. Once Baker notified an undertaker 30 miles away in Cottonwood Falls, ambulances rushed to the scene over muddy roads, which slowed their travel time to a crawl.

By the time ambulances arrived, word of the crash had already spread like wildfire throughout the area. Crowds of locals, drawn to the site by morbid curiosity, snatched up bits of the plane. Large pieces of the wing, fuselage, and other significant plane parts that might have otherwise revealed the actual cause of the crash were loaded as souvenirs into cars and pickup trucks.

Some locals got in and out of the crash scene quickly enough to make their way to hotel lobbies in nearby towns and sell the wreckage souvenirs before ambulances carrying the morticians and caskets arrived from Cottonwood Falls to collect the remains of Rockne and the rest of the victims.

Christen's body was found with $400 in his clothes. Just two days later on April 2, newspapers across the country reported that mystery surrounded the disappearance of $55,000 Christen was said to have withdrawn shortly before boarding the plane. His attorney, Murray Miller, reasoned that Christen could have deposited the money in another bank or invested it in securities before he left for the trip. The possibility of a souvenir collector coming across the money wrapped in a briefcase or similar pack and running off with a cash windfall amid the onset of the Great Depression was never mentioned in newspaper follow-ups.

Harold V. Lyle, a rookie photographer for the Wichita Eagle, had previously met Rockne in Newton, Kansas, when the coach and the Notre Dame football team were eating breakfast while waiting for a train. When Lyle arrived at the Eagle office early on the morning of March 31, he was greeted by a brief teletype saying Rockne had left Kansas City on a Transcontinental & Western flight bound for Wichita. It didn't take long for the bulletin bell on the teletype machine to ring with a wire report of a plane going down in Chase County, Kansas.

Lyle and the newspaper's sports editor, Bill Cunningham, immediately chartered a plane and headed to the area. Their pilot couldn't locate the wreckage from the air until he spotted a cowboy on the ground wearing a red bandana on a horse waving them toward the southeast. Once over the wreckage, Lyle snapped photos of the tail and the devastation of plane wreckage surrounded by a large gathering of people and several black cars. He also shot photos of circular tracks of tire trails in the snow left behind by local souvenir scavengers who had snatched pieces of the wrecked plane and taken off.

"I knew then, by the size of the airplane, it was the Transcontinental and Western," Lyle recalled 37 years later on the anniversary of the crash. "I knew Rockne was dead. I took the aerial photographs then. I hated to, but it was my job."

Since nobody knew the identities of the eight victims, responders on the ground could only ask one question: How did it happen?

The Associated Press was the first news outlet to break the story. Every late edition of every newspaper across the country, which printed the AP account of the crash on March 31, 1931, cited witnesses on the ground who heard an "explosion" in mid-air. Several newspapers reported eyewitness accounts that saw the plane "in flames" as it "cartwheeled" to the ground.

Same-day headlines screamed "Explosion!" on the front pages of both afternoon editions in Pittsburgh. "Knute Rockne, 7 Others Die As Plane Explodes, Crashes," blared the Pittsburgh (Pa.) Sun Telegraph. "Knute Rockne, 7 Others Die As Plane Explodes," echoed The Pittsburgh (Pa.) Press. A bold-highlighted subhead on the front-page crash story in the Red Bluff (California) Daily News revealed "Explosion on Plane Reported By Farmer Watching Flight," then cited Edward Baker's eyewitness account with the description: "Suddenly, he said, there was an explosion and the ship fell to the earth."

Three hours later when crash investigators from the Aeronautics Branch of the U.S. Commerce Department arrived on the scene, details of the plane coming down began to soften from the first "explosion" accounts. The following day, newspapers made no mention of a mid-air explosion. "Wing Drops From Clouds, Plane Falls," the New York Daily News headline announced on April 1, 1931.

The version told by the property's owner, Steward Baker, differed slightly from his son's on-the-spot eyewitness recollection of hearing an "explosion" in mid-air and the plane "falling in flames" from the sky.

"We heard the plane flying over this morning, but couldn't see it for the clouds," Steward Baker said in nationwide reports that splashed headlines of the plane crash the following morning. "A minute later it sounded like the motors were missing and then we couldn't hear them at all. It seemed like five minutes after the ship passed over the house that we heard the crash. It landed in the pasture about a mile from the house and when it hit, it sounded like a muffled explosion. It didn't catch fire after it hit."

Some newspapers were quick to report investigators' claims that ice on the wings brought the plane down. Other newspapers indicated that the pilot's visibility was blinded by clouds, and that the plane's instruments had been rendered useless by ice that formed on the wing's air tubes. When the pilot realized the plane was in a death spiral, it was too late, and part of a wing pulled off when he tried to pull out of the dive, reports speculated.

News conjectures were countered by eyewitnesses on the ground and air traffic controllers in Wichita who claimed the pilots knew where they were. Weather conditions were not ideal, but Wichita airport's radar system showed no signs of severe weather systems.

Also noted was a NAT Mail plane piloted by Paul E. Johnson that flew safely without any problems just ahead of the Fokker F-10. A preliminary investigation revealed that although temperatures were slightly above freezing on the ground, no ice had been found on any part of the plane.

10

IDENTIFICATIONS

Word leaked out that Rockne's name was listed on the flight log's passenger list.

The press not only had a national disaster to report, but also that the most famous football coach in America was among the dead. Every newspaper and radio network across the country jumped on the news that Rockne was killed before the coroner confirmed the identities of any of the victims.

In a fateful twist of irony, Jess Harper, the former Notre Dame coach Rockne replaced in 1918, was living about 100 miles away from the crash site. Harper heard the news, jumped in his car and drove to Cottonwood Falls to officially identify his longtime friend's body.

Martha Gjermo Rockne learned of her son's death from a radio news bulletin, as did Martha Stiles, one of Rockne's four sisters. Mrs. Stiles phoned WGN Radio in Chicago for an update, but she was told her brother's body had not yet been identified; the station was still awaiting confirmation.

When the news was confirmed to Martha Rockne that her son was among the dead, her calm words were spiritually subdued: "It's God's will and we must not question it."

Martha snapped off a cable to Bonnie Rockne, who was still in Florida. But Bonnie never received the wire from her mother-in-law. She was at the beach spending her last day in Florida with daughter Mary Jeanne, and Tom O'Neil and his wife, the Rocknes' friends from Akron, Ohio.

At about 2:30 p.m., Bonnie and Mary Jean rode in a car with the O'Neils back to the house in Coral Gables, where a handful of friends had gathered along with telegrams that began to arrive offering condolences. O'Neil no sooner pulled the car into a garage when an attendant recognized Bonnie. The attendant pulled O'Neil aside and told him about the crash.

Shocked and devastated, O'Neil maintained his composure long enough to approach Bonnie. "I've got some serious news for you," he said gently.

A look of disbelief crossed Bonnie's face. No way her husband was dead. Just a few hours ago she received the telegram Knute had wired before he boarded the plane in Kansas City.

"LEAVING RIGHT NOW WILL BE AT BILTMORE LOVE AND KISSES... KNUTE." were Rockne's last words to his wife.

"I just don't believe it," Bonnie repeated softly, over and over. Only after sitting down with O'Neil and a priest, Father David Barry of Miami Beach, did Bonnie accept the tragic news as fact.

She turned to her son, Jackie. "Your daddy has gone away. He loved you so."

*Bonnie put forth a brave face. With urgency to help her family pack for the long trip back to South Bend, Bonnie began to fill an old trunk with the initials "K.K.R." printed inside. Among the items Bonnie made sure to take home included the small football Knute and little Jackie kicked around the front yard before he left. The trunk was nearly filled, with barely enough space for the ball. Over Neil's suggestion to let the air out of the ball, Bonnie made room for her husband's last bastion of life without deflating it.

"Knute blew that up himself," she said.

Chicago Tribune Sports Editor Arch Ward had spoken with Rockne over the phone earlier that morning before the coach boarded the plane in Kansas City. Ward was at his home in Chicago when he received a call from Tribune Managing Editor Loy Maloney.

"Where's your friend, Rockne?" Maloney asked. "There's a report that this might be the plane he was on. You better get down here. There's nothing official, but it looks like Knute Rockne's dead."

Ward was stunned. Rockne's passionate voice talking about his plans to take a jazz band on a tour of Europe to raise money for the cancer-stricken mother of one of his players was still fresh in Ward's head. Rockne had also mentioned that Hearst newspapers were offering to pay him $75,000 to retire from coaching and write a syndicated football column.

Ward had hung up the phone from Rockne thrilled over the thought that prosperity was finally on the horizon for his friend, a beloved icon who had given away more money to help people in need than he had ever made coaching at Notre Dame. Rockne's sudden death was no mere tragedy – it was a paralyzing injustice.

Ward picked up the phone and dialed the number at the Rockne's vacation home in Coral Gables. Bonnie answered.

"Mrs. Rockne, there's this crazy story going around," Ward said. "I don't mean to upset you, but the wire services think something awful has happened to Rock."

"It's true," Bonnie replied. "They just called."

The phone clicked off in Ward's ear.

That night, Bonnie, Mary Jeanne, Jackie, the O'Neils and the Rocknes' maid caught the train. The ride was a long, somber trip home.

Word of Rockne's death spread like wildfire throughout Notre Dame and South Bend. "Have you heard?" was a question that started every conversation on campus prompting the common reply, "Can it really be true?" As initial reports confirmed the death, the Basilica of the Sacred Heart filled up quickly with a stream of students, faculty members and campus workers, many crying openly. Telephone lines were flooded with students calling family members to relay the tragic news.

Eugene "Scrapiron" Young, the first full-time trainer in Notre Dame history, left his home at around 1 p.m. Strolling along Eddy Street Road toward the campus two blocks into his walk, Young heard footsteps approaching. He turned to see who might be running to catch up. One of Rockne's players, John "Big John" McManmon, lumbered toward Young at a fast speed before he stopped next to the trainer huffing to catch his breath.

"Have you heard, Scrap?" Big John's usual jovial Irish nature had submitted to a voice that sounded like it was coming from a tomb.

"Have I heard what?" Young asked, expecting McManmon to break into one of his customary practical jokes.

"Oh, dear God," McManmon said. "I hope it isn't true. They say Rock is dead."

Young's heart stopped beating. His legs sagged. A cold chill formed in his toes and shot upwards through his body like a lightning bolt that pierced his brain.

"Dead!" Young gasped, looking directly into McManmon's eyes. Genuine horror was etched in Big John's face.

McManmon filled Young in on the sketchy details of what had been reported of the crash. The two headed over to the Administration Building, taking the steps two at a time. When they got to the door of the Athletic Office both froze in their tracks. Young's stomach contracted into what felt like a fist-like knot. Bracing themselves as best as they could, Young and Big John entered the office.

Rockne's assistants had already gathered in the Athletic Office. Hunk Anderson, Jack Chevigny, Ike Voedisch and Tim Moynihan talked quietly amongst themselves. Rockne's secretary, Ruth Faulkner, wept openly.

News spread throughout campus as the seconds turned to minutes. Phones rang occasionally at first, then rapidly became an incessant clamor of calls from newspapermen and radio stations from around the country. People crowded into the Athletic Office, including the football team. Players' emotions ran the gamut. Some talked excitedly, while others tried to whisper quietly. Others clenched fists and alternated pacing the floor pounding their fists into their hands or against the wall. Some just stood and prayed.

The office door opened and the secretary to Notre Dame President Father Charles L. O'Donnell entered the room. "Will you all please follow me?" she asked.

Young followed the team and everyone else into the president's office where Father O'Donnell was waiting. He waited until the last team member arrived then closed the door. Father O'Donnell removed his glasses; Young noticed red-rimmed eyes.

"Gentlemen, we have lost the best friend that a man could ever have," is all Father O'Donnell could say before his voice broke on the last word. The only sound in the room was the sobs of players.

Father Reynolds was supervising a recreation period with students when the news hit. He dropped to his knees. His body went numb. The priest listened in silent shock as radio reports told of an eyewitness, "a little farmer boy," who heard an explosion in the clouds and watched "a pillar of fire rise up near where the wing attached itself to the machine... and then the wing flew off..."

It was all Father Reynolds could do to bow his head in prayer.

11

GUILTY

Two days after the crash, headlines of Rockne's death and tributes to his remarkable life and coaching career overshadowed the end to what had been the biggest story in Chicago for the better part of the year:

After three weeks of witnesses testifying at Cook County Criminal Court in the high-profile trial formally entitled "The State of Illinois vs. Leo V. Brothers," a jury found Leo Brothers guilty of murdering Jake Lingle.

The Brothers' trial, which lasted from March 16 to April 2, nearly ended in a hung jury because of evidence that had been just as evenly balanced in Brothers' favor as it was against him. The jury deliberated 27 hours before coming back with what many viewed as a compromised verdict – a guilty verdict that would be challenged unsuccessfully a year later in Brothers' appeal to the Illinois State Supreme Court titled "The People v Brothers."

"The principal controversy relates to the identification of (Brothers) as the man who shot Lingle and fled from the scene of the crime," Illinois State Supreme Court Justice Norman L. Jones wrote in his lead opinion filed in response to defense attorney Louis Piquett's appeal in February 1932. "Various witnesses positively identified defendant as being in the tunnel and as the man who dropped the gun and ran up the stairs and across the street. Other witnesses testified with equal positiveness that they were present and that defendant was not that man."

Of six prosecution witnesses, five positively identified Brothers as the man they had seen run from the tunnel of the train station and flee across Michigan Avenue. Warren Williams, Daniel Davidson Mills, Marcus David, and Patrick Campbell – the man who bumped into Father Reynolds as he started to chase the assailant – each testified that they got a good look at Brothers' face. Williams claimed the man passed within a foot of him as he ran out.

Otto Swoboda told jurors that he was in the public library shortly before the shooting and noticed a man, whom he later learned was Frankie Foster, leaning against the wall of the library with another man standing nearby. A short while later as Swoboda was crossing the street to go to Grant Park, he walked into the tunnel when a man rushed past him and knocked a lighted cigarette out of his mouth. Swoboda testified that he recognized Brothers as the man who had knocked his cigarette out.

Red flags popped up on these prosecution witnesses as soon as the trial began. Swoboda had been paid by the state attorney sums ranging from $2 to $25 on several occasions.

And he had been compensated to travel to two out-of-state prisons where Brothers was held, including Leavenworth, which bordered on prosecutorial witness tampering.

Williams was on the payroll of the state attorney's office as an investigator to the tune of $200 a month. Campbell — known by two names, Patrick and John — was free on $2,500 Cook County bond for conspiracy to commit robbery. Campbell had also been working on a plea deal with the same Cook County prosecutor's office when he was called to testify against Brothers.

Chicago Police Officer Anthony Ruthy had followed one of the suspects out of the train station onto Michigan Avenue. Ruthy initially identified Frankie Foster as the man he had chased. But when he took the witness stand and it came out that he was mentally unbalanced due to a previous brain injury, and that he had been assigned by the Police Department to light duty at the time of the Lingle murder, Ruthy was ruled to be unreliable and his testimony was suppressed.

Seven witnesses with no strings attached to either the defense or prosecution freely testified that Brothers was not the gunman.

Lawrence O'Malley, a railroad switchman, said he was in the underpass "within six feet" of the triggerman when Lingle was shot. Brothers, O'Malley claimed, was not the shooter. Real estate broker Harry J. O'Connor, who was in the tunnel when he heard the shot, told both sides of attorneys that he could not identify Brothers as the assailant. Albert Stein, an employee in the Cook County Office of the Recorder, was with O'Connor and another man in the tunnel at Randolph Street when he heard a gunshot and saw a man running with two men chasing him up the stairs. Stein told jurors the man he saw was "not as tall, or as heavy," as Brothers.

Abigail Wilson, Madeline Whitehurst, Paul Thomas and Pasquale Clarizio each testified to seeing the gunman running away – but they didn't see the defendant. Whitehurst told jurors that she "got a good look" at a "young man coming up the stairs" at the same time she heard someone in the tunnel shouting, "Get that man!" She told jurors that she had never seen the man before in her life — and that she had never seen Brothers before the day of the trial. Clarizio, a stock clerk with the Dennison Manufacturing Company at 62 East Randolph Street, recalled seeing Officer Ruthy and several people chasing a man through an alley. Brothers, Clarizio maintained, was not the man Ruthy was chasing.

Despite the witnesses' denials under oath in front of the judge and jury, Leo Brothers was found guilty of pulling the trigger on Lingle.

Conviction of first-degree murder called for the death penalty. Yet, Brothers was sentenced to 14 years in prison, a sentence commutable to eight years for good behavior. As the rest of the country mourned Rockne's death, Brothers laughed off the light sentence.

"I can do that standing on my head," Brothers boasted with a smirk.

Post-trial newspaper accounts revealed that prosecutors, police, Chicago politicians and even the

Chicago Tribune considered Brothers' conviction as a turning point in the city's battle with gangsters.

In the months after the Lingle murder, the city's top brass found themselves on the receiving end of heavy public backlash screaming that criminals, namely Capone, were ruling the city through violence. The same law enforcement bosses and high-end politicos who lauded the Brothers conviction as a big win for the city were the same figureheads who manipulated circumstances surrounding the trial so Brothers could be convicted in the Lingle murder and give the public what it was clamoring for: a guilty verdict and closure to a high-profile case.

Among all the witnesses to take the stand, only Father Reynolds had seen the actual gunman pull the trigger. When he took the stand on March 27, the priest remained ambivalent in his identification of Brothers. The priest testified to seeing a "blond young chap with a gray suit and blond hair" running from the tunnel between "the safety island and the curb" while being chased by a policeman.

"Do you see anyone in the courtroom now that you saw that day?" prosecutor Curly Brooks asked.

"Mr. Brothers answers the description," Father Reynolds carefully replied.

Brothers attorney, Louis Piquett, never pressed Father Reynolds for clarity. The priest's nebulous choice of words left the question of "reasonable doubt" open for the jury to mull, which satisfied the defense lawyer who made a nice living defending gangsters in Capone's crew and, later, John Dillinger. Father Reynolds' fuzzy description that left Brothers' guilt or innocence wide open for interpretation was also satisfactory to the judge, the prosecutors, and everyone else in the courtroom, including the press.

Brothers was a formidable sacrificial lamb. During the months prior to the trial during questioning of suspects, investigators learned that St. Louis mobster Fred Burke, a former charter member of Egan's Rats, had hired Lingle's killers. It was Burke who brought in Brothers to don a different disguise each day and trail the Tribune reporter to get an idea of his schedule so the hit could be planned with a time and place. On at least one occasion, Brothers had followed Lingle disguised as a priest.

Brothers may not have pulled the trigger, but he had been involved in the murderous conspiracy. That was good enough for city officials determined to secure a conviction in a high-profile case and save face in a city where an outraged public demanded protection against organized crime.

Capone, meanwhile, continued to be the subject of a growing investigation into his finances by the IRS. Several of Capone's friends and associates on his payroll, including politicians and reporters such as Jake Lingle, maintained intimate knowledge of the gangster's illegal financial sources - most notably from bootlegging, gambling and prostitution. If Capone went down for not paying taxes, politicians and anyone else connected to his illegal enterprise would go with him.

Politicians aligned with Capone needed his help in putting Brothers forward (and paying for his high-priced defense attorney) to make everybody look good in the public's eye. Convicting Brothers was beneficial to both city officials and Capone, who was able to protect his close confidant and crew member, Frankie Foster, the man Father Reynolds positively identified as the actual gunman.

Father Reynolds could have easily turned the whole plan to convict Brothers upside down. The priest remained ambivalent on the stand, yet still managed to skirt the edge of truth. But how much longer could he remain quiet while Brothers served his nominal time in prison? There was a lot at stake for the most powerful people in Chicago, and it was riding on a conviction of Brothers that would put the entire public relations nightmare to bed once and for all.

If only Father Reynolds had buckled to the intimidation tactics and stayed at Notre Dame. Instead, a holy linchpin got off the witness stand, walked out of court and caught the first train back to South Bend with a bull's eye on his back.

Four weeks after Brothers entered the penitentiary to begin serving his sentence, two boys found the charred remains of an old brothel keeper who had been demoted to a relatively minuscule position in the Capone organization. Angry and resentful before he was murdered and his car set on fire, Mike de Pike Heitler had fired off an anonymous letter to State Attorney John Swanson disclosing everything he knew about Capone's bordello operations.

In a second letter to his daughter, Heitler expanded on the information he penned to the State's Attorney. The letter also included instructions to deliver to Pat Roche for use as evidence in the Brothers trial, but the posthumous testimony proved too obscure for the judge to admit so a jury could hear.

Heitler's correspondence did strengthen what investigators had suspected all along. The letter named eight gangsters who had conspired to kill Jake Lingle, all members of Capone's crew, and he described a meeting where Capone lambasted Lingle as a double-crosser.

"Jake…" Heitler quoted Capone as promising, "… is going to get his."

Several years later, Johnny Roselli, a Capone affiliate famously known as "Handsome Johnny" who had moved to Los Angeles soon after the Lingle murder where he became one of the most influential mob muscles in Hollywood, put the final stamp on speculation as to who had actually pulled the trigger on Jake Lingle.

Roselli named Frankie Foster and Ted Newberry as the true killers of Jake Lingle.

12

FUNERAL FOR AN ICON

D r. Michael Nigro took it upon himself to gather

Rockne's physical remains in Kansas City and assemble them in the casket. He drove Billy and Knute Jr. out to see the crash site where their father had died, then returned to the train station in Kansas City to accompany the boys and the casket on the long ride back to South Bend.

Billy and Knute Jr. were in a state of confusion. Because their train was late getting back from Florida, they had missed seeing their father for the last time by mere minutes. Now, the two young boys, 14 and 11, stood reluctantly alongside Dr. Nigro, Jess Harper and other strangers who knew their famous dad, posing for insistent newspaper photographers seemingly paralyzed in dazed, grief-stricken silence.

The train pulled out of Kansas City early Thursday morning on the prayers of a shocked country engulfed in a national outpouring of grief usually reserved for the death of a president. President Herbert Hoover called Rockne's death "a national loss." King Haakon VII of Norway posthumously knighted Norway's favorite son and sent a personal envoy to Rockne's massive funeral.

The train from Kansas City rolled into Chicago Thursday at 7:45 p.m. Floral arrangements and tributes flooded the Chicago residence of Rockne's mother, Martha Rockne, who had already traveled to South Bend to be with her son's family at their home on Wayne Street in the city's Sunnymede section. Following a brief stop in Chicago, the train was back on the rails carrying Rockne's casket to his final resting place in South Bend.

Out of respect for the legendary Notre Dame coach, Charles H. Jones, general manager of the South Shore railway line, announced that all trains and motor coaches of the Chicago South Shore and South Bend railroad would be halted for one minute at the hour of the Rockne funeral services.

At the request of Bonnie Rockne, the funeral was set for 4:30 p.m. on Saturday – the day before Easter – despite the Catholic Church's dictum that no funeral could be said on Holy Thursday, Good Friday, Holy Saturday or Easter Sunday.

Thousands showed up Saturday morning at the Rocknes' simple brick home on Wayne Street to view the casket holding Rockne's body situated somberly near his fireplace. The casket remained closed, another decision made by Bonnie Rockne due to the severity of her husband's injuries.

Among the roster of guests – a virtual "Who's Who" of notables from the sporting and coaching world plus a cavalcade of prominent politicians and statesmen – included New York Mayor James Walker, who was returning from Los Angeles and ordered his special car to stop in South Bend so he could pay his final respects. The mayor of New York City did not forget the man who had assembled a team of Notre Dame stars from past years to play an unemployment benefit football game in New York.

"My words would be worthless if I were not speaking for 60,000 families whose wage-earners, out of work, had been materially aided by the charity game last winter," Walker said in an impromptu eulogy. "Knute Rockne came clear from California, where he had closed a glorious season, and at the risk of his personal health gathered the team that battled for charity on a cold and forbidding day. New York recognizes the benefactions his life has made in the training of manhood, but it realizes with an unforgettable memory the service this man gave to us in a time of need."

South Bend City Hall and Notre Dame's campus were draped in black. Flags of the city fluttered in the breeze at half-mast. Business was shut down as University and municipal authorities made funeral preparations while trying to convince themselves that their city's national icon was gone. Cab drivers solemnly asked passengers if they had come to the city for the funeral while recalling tales of driving football fans to the train stations to greet Rockne's

Notre Dame teams. Hotel porters lingered obliviously over routine duties, speaking instead of banquets and meetings the coach attended.

"People have heard so much about his speed and dash that they think he must have been unreasonable," one hotel porter reminisced to the Indianapolis Star. "He wasn't. I have seen the time he wouldn't let me bother the manager of the hotel until his turn came to be admitted, and he just sat on the davenport and waited, smiling. And you never heard of Rockne snubbing anybody."

At 2 p.m., Rockne's casket was loaded into the back of the funeral car and taken from his home on a solemn cortege through the streets of South Bend. Lining bedecked roadways, thousands stood bare-headed in reverence as the procession rolled by. As it passed Notre Dame Stadium, the grandiose football mecca Rockne himself had built, there was a silent pause cast in solemn salute.

Grief spread from South Bend to Chicago, stretched from coast to coast, and was felt abroad from Australia to Rockne's native Norway — a magnanimous sendoff normally reserved for a president, king or statesman that prompted press accounts to openly question whether Rockne had gained the largest personal following of any man in the United States at the time.

A lone sound rang through the air. The great bell of Notre Dame's picturesque Gothic Basilica of the Sacred Heart tolled solemnly as students and faculty knelt before the altar. Father O'Donnell, president of Notre Dame University, celebrated mass and gave communion to every Catholic student in attendance.

The funeral service inside Sacred Heart was limited to 1,400 members of Rockne's intimate circle. In its span of more than 60 years, Sacred Heart had been the scene of numerous services for Notre Dame's beloved, but none of those previous services came close to approaching the impressiveness, sadness or sorrow over the loss of the iconic Notre Dame football coach.

Rockne's mother, mere days past her 72nd birthday, sat with his children, Billy, Knute Jr., Mary Jeanne and Jackie, along with Rockne's four sisters. Bonnie passed through the solemn crowd on the arms of Notre Dame Assistant Coach Jack Chevigny and Dr. Nigro.

As the choir sang "Popule Meus," the casket was wheeled to the foot of the altar for final blessings administered by a trio of priests – Bishop John F. Noll of the Fort Wayne diocese; the Rev. Thomas Steiner, C.S.C., dean of the school of engineering; and the Rev. John F. O'Hara, C.S.C., prefect of religion. The Rev. William Connor, C.S.C., served as master of ceremonies.

Father O'Donnell's eulogy rang out through the church.

"He was a man of the people. A husband and father, a citizen of South Bend, Indiana. Yet, had he been any one of these personages that have been mentioned, the tributes of admiration and affection which he has received could not be more universal or more sincere."

The same group of "Ramblers" who carried Rockne's teams to football glory on the field carried his casket out of Sacred Heart and loaded it into the funeral car for the final two-and-a-half-mile leg of Knute Rockne's extraordinary journey on earth. Tommy Conley, Tommy Yarr, Marchmont Schwartz, Frank Carideo, Marty Brill and Larry Mullins each wept openly as they tenderly embraced their immortal leader's ravaged remains and carried the casket from the hearse to his final resting place beneath the spreading branches of Old Council Oak's Highland Cemetery. The St. Joseph River flowed peacefully nearby.

It was a simple farewell carried out by the boys who fought for him on the field and blessed by the holy fathers with whom he had worked and worshipped. It was a final procession that gripped the heartstrings of Notre Dame, colleagues, rivals, a stunned nation, and a world that shed profound tears in collective grief when Rockne's casket was lowered into the ground.

Two thousand miles away, Robert "Joe-Pete" Fry, a 32-year-old former military pilot who flew several recon missions for the Marines in China just four years prior, was also laid to rest in Los Angeles. The TWA pilot's bride of only eight months, Mary Breeden Fry, and his parents, Mr. and Mrs. John Fry of Milwaukee, were among the few present at Fry's military funeral.

Rockne, Fry and the six others who perished in the plane crash felt 'round the world' were all laid to rest in eternal peace. The cause of the crash, however, did not rest at all with the Aeronautics Branch of the Department of Commerce.

13

PAYBACK

Father Reynolds remained hopeful that The Chicago Tribune would pay him at least $25,000 in reward money for his part in the arrest and conviction of Lingle's killer. The only money he'd seen so far was $25 in expense money shelled out by police and prosecutors when they had called him to Chicago to view a suspect.

The expense money was all he would get. Nine months of dodging mobsters' threats, traveling to and from Chicago to view police photographs of suspects, risking life and limb to testify in a pressure-cooked trial, praying for strength every minute of every day, and wracking himself with guilt after hearing the news that his friend Rockne had been killed on the very airplane he should've been on... would wind up being worth $25.

"There was a $25,000 reward by the Tribune; they were trying to cover up, I think, for the one who would help to arrest, get the one who did the killing arrested and help to convict them, see..." Father Reynolds said. "But after time was over, there was a Notre Dame boy in charge of the program for the Tribune. I phoned him and said, 'How about the $25,000? Because my testimony kind of put the trial over, see?'

"And he said, 'Well, you got your share of all those trips you came in when we paid you $25 and it only cost you $2 to come in.'"

Father Reynolds hung up the phone. If anyone needed a spiritual course in upholding the truth, it was the folks responsible for convicting Leo Brothers in a murder actually committed by Frankie Foster.

"See, I wouldn't tell them that he was the man. I told them plainly that if I couldn't get any other better-looking character than him to fulfill the characteristics of the man I saw running away, I would take him, see?"

The Chicago Tribune paid out $25,000 to an undisclosed source in total confidentiality through the Illinois State Attorney General's Office. The Chicago Herald-Examiner added $25,000 to the reward pot, and the Chicago Evening Post kicked in another $5,000, for a total of $55,000.

Within two days of the Rockne crash, newspapers splashed reports that one of the victims, H.J. Christen, an interior designer in Chicago who earned a modest living setting up floor fixtures for downtown department and sporting goods stores, had cashed a check for $55,000 the day before boarding the plane. Crash responders found only $400 in Christen's clothes when his body was recovered.

The post-crash spotlight fell on a bigger inquisition: How did newspaper editors know immediately to report in first-day accounts that a modest interior designer named H.J. Christen, a virtual nobody in the world of fame and fortune occupied by Knute Rockne, had cashed a check for $55,000 one day before the plane went down? Was it coincidence, that $55,000 was the same combined amount paid out by their own employers?

And for whom was the money earmarked? Christen? Could Christen have been a bag carrier flying under the radar of vengeful mobsters to deliver the reward money to its rightful benefactor in a place far away from Chicago where the transaction could be conducted out of sight and mind?

It was unlikely that the reward money was for Rockne. But Rockne had been traveling with John Happer, comptroller for Great Western Sporting Goods, another victim of the crash. Did Christen have a business relationship setting up floor fixtures for Happer's sporting goods store in Chicago? Could the two have been flying to Los Angeles with Rockne to set up a new Great Western Sporting Goods Store? Or was there other, more covert business planned? Christen and Happer were the only two actual residents of Chicago flying on that plane.

How Christen obtained $55,000 was a question that died unanswered in the crash with him.

Father Reynolds moved forward with his life at Notre Dame teaching American History and serving as rector at St. Edward's Hall. He wanted nothing more than to serve his students and live quietly in a spiritual manner in the aftermath of the trial and the crash that had killed his beloved friend. Simply, he had had enough.

Two years later, Father Reynolds got hit with another blast of public notoriety.

On a cold January afternoon just after the turn of 1933, the priest was hanging out in a bar in South Bend drinking beers with a few friends. Their conversation was drowned out by loud calls of a newsie boy out on the street hawking the day's edition of the South Bend News-Times. Father Reynolds had just taken a swig of beer when his gulp was interrupted by the sound of the newsboy shouting his name outside.

"Read all about it! Special edition! The underworld tried to kill Father Reynolds!"

According to the News-Times, an "unimpeachable source" told the newspaper the federal Secret Service was investigating reports that a bomb had caused the Fokker Trimotor aircraft to crash and kill Rockne, five other passengers and the two pilots.

On Jan. 6, 1933, a headline in the Washington Times blared: "Rockne Died Gangsters' Victim."

The Washington Times story echoed the South Bend News-Times account: A bomb planted on the plane was meant for Father Reynolds in retaliation for his testifying in the Brothers' trial.

"This is the first I have heard of such an astonishing angle in the tragedy," Major John Griffith, commissioner of the Big Ten Conference and head of the Coaches Association, was quoted as saying in the Washington Times article. "I hope, and I'm sure all other lovers of football hope that if it is true that gangsters were responsible, the government captures them and gives them the punishment they deserve."

The following day, Jan. 7, 1933, headlines put the South Bend News-Time's exclusive on full blast in newspapers across the country.

"BOMB KILLED ROCKNE, PUT IN PLANE BY GANG," screamed the Detroit Evening Times over an underlying subhead that rocked the sports world from Rockne's grave.

"Government operatives were in South Bend this week investigating several angles of the case. It was reported they were working with airline officials in the hope of getting some traces of the mobsters who were believed to have caused the plane crash."

The Evening Times' story concluded that Father Reynolds was at the forefront of the investigation.

"Father Reynolds was an important witness at the trial of Leo V. Brothers, who was convicted of the sensational Lingle slaying and was sentenced to 14 years in the state penitentiary. Credence was given to the theory that Rockne's plane was wrecked by a bomb when it was recalled that witnesses declared a violent explosion preceded the crash."

The Santa Ana (Calif.) Register story delved even further into who actually planted the bomb under the headline, "Claim Rockne Air Crash Due to Gangster's Bomb."

"Secret Service operatives were in South Bend a few days ago rounding out their evidence... and had it complete even to the name of the man suspected of placing the bomb in a mail pouch in the plane," the Register reported in its Jan. 6, 1933 edition.

"The name of the suspect was not revealed to our informant, the (South Bend) News Times said."

Father Reynolds took another gulp of beer. The shocking news of the day was what the priest had suspected all along.

Neither the New York Times nor the Chicago Tribune were certain enough to run the story. Both newspapers contacted the FBI to see if a government investigation was being conducted into the crash. Indiana Congressman Samuel Pettingill, representing the state's 3rd Congressional District, also reached out to the FBI to inquire about a federal probe.

One FBI agent denied the existence of any investigation to The New York Times. The Tribune was told that the publicity spokesman the paper needed to speak with "could not be reached." J. Edgar Hoover himself responded to the congressman's query indirectly through another FBI agent. The FBI director's note to the agent passed on to Pettingill did not completely deny the investigation.

"I said we were not conducting any investigation of this, insofar as I knew or had been advised," Hoover replied in a memo, "but that I understood the investigation was being made by the Commerce Department."

Two days after the Rockne crash's mob-linked headlines were splashed across the country, the body of Edward "Ted" Newberry was discovered on a lonely stretch of road in Indiana, south of the Chicago line. Found around the waist of Newberry's body was a belt with a diamond studded belt buckle. Like the similar one flaunted by Jake Lingle, Newberry's belt buckle had also been a gift from Al Capone.

"He must have done something," Newberry once said of a murder victim. "They don't kill you for nothing."

14

MADE IN HOLLYWOOD

T he news that a gangster's bomb may have been linked to the Rockne plane crash barely lasted two days before it died out.

By 1933, most of the country's populace had two years to recover from the collective grief of Rockne's death. More important concerns crippled Americans devastated by the height of the Great Depression. And in Germany, a notorious dictator was rounding up Jews and putting them in death camps while his Nazi military gained strength by the day and threatened to throw the entire world into an earth-shattering war.

One evening in 1934, Notre Dame sophomore James Bacon was hanging out with pal and Notre Dame football captain Kitty Gorman drinking beer with the rector of St.

Edward's Hall where Bacon and Gorman resided as roommates. Bacon would later move to California and establish himself as one of Hollywood's most notable newspaper columnists. In his 1977 book, "Made in Hollywood," Bacon recalled that Gorman was the football team's center and a favorite student among Notre Dame priests because he was a Minim.

Gorman grew up attending school through the Notre Dame Minims, once the elementary and high-school branch of Notre Dame, before entering the University of Notre Dame. Being one of the few Minims still left at Notre Dave provided Gorman with privileged and exclusive friendships with the university's priests not afforded to other students. Gorman was frequently welcomed to hang out and drink beer with the rector of St. Edward's Hall, Father John Reynolds, even though the drinking of alcohol by students on campus was a strict violation of campus rules.

"So that explains how I was in the rector's office drinking beer," Bacon wrote in his book. "I came with Kitty."

That night over beer and chitchat, Father Reynolds made small talk before he slid into an astonishing tale that stunned the two awestruck students — a story that began in the early afternoon of June 9, 1930, when he administered the last rites of the Catholic Church to a Chicago Tribune reporter by the name of Jake Lingle.

The boys listened intently as Father Reynolds put them in Lingle's shoes — leaving the Sherman House Hotel to catch the 1:30 p.m. train to a racetrack in Homewood where Lingle was planning to lay bets on the horses. They were all ears as the priest walked Lingle toward the Illinois Central platform at the foot of Randolph Street, where Lingle noticed he was being followed by two men.

There was a blond man with blue eyes in a straw hat who fumbled a .38 caliber pistol., the priest recalled vividly. And there was a short, stocky, dark-haired man who snatched the gun and fired a bullet into the back of Lingle's head.

Father Reynolds explained how he rushed to the mortally wounded Lingle just in time to give him last rites … how Lingle barely whispered something in the priest's ear before he took his final breath.

Father Reynolds told the boys he remembered the exact words Lingle whispered. Those words, he insisted, would forever remain between Lingle, Father Reynolds and God.

Bacon and Gorman sat spellbound as Father Reynolds recounted testifying in the Brothers' trial. He recalled being caught between pressure by police to testify against Brothers, and enduring months of threats and intimidation tactics from underworld figures lurking in the shadows outside his residence at Morrissey Hall, trying to keep him from testifying.

"Father Reynolds then told Kitty and me a horrendous tale of his harassment by gangsters, all of whom wanted to know what Lingle had divulged to him during that last confession," Bacon penned in "Made in Hollywood."

The priest informed the two students that he had given every inquisitive mobster the same answer: He was bound by the seal of confessional to keep Lingle's final confession to himself. The longer Father Reynolds stayed tight-lipped about the confession, the more phone calls and mysterious visits from shady characters he had received.

The priest shifted his recollection to his friend, Knute Rockne. Gorman and Bacon sat in silence.

"Father Reynolds told us, 'My name was on Rock's tickets and reservation. He didn't have time to change them. And then all those threats on my life. Did those people plant a bomb on that plane for me? I don't know.

"I know if I hadn't given Rock my tickets, he would have been alive."

Section 3: The Investigation

15

PUBLIC DEMAND

"First reports were that the plane exploded."

The magnitude of that single line of seven words documented on page 16 of the Aeronautics Branch of the U.S. Department of Commerce's official investigation report into the crash of Transcontinental & Western Air Flight 5 that killed Knute Rockne and seven others cannot be understated.

Just a few hours after the crash occurred at about 10:45 a.m. on the morning of March 31, 1931, newspapers across the country ran their first, on-the-spot breaking news stories. All quoted young Edward Baker saying he heard the Fokker F-10A "explode in the air" and "spin in flames" as it crashed to the ground in a pasture on his father's rural Kansas ranch.

Just as news of the crash began pinging teletype and telegraph wire services, news reporters and photographers throughout Kansas grabbed equipment, hopped in cars or on charter planes, and headed to the remote site at the edge of the state's rugged Flint Hills to interview witnesses and get the first details of the tragedy. Edward Baker, his brother Arthur Baker, Clarence H. McCracken, R.C. Blackburn, Easter Heathman and members of the Heathman family all gave emotional eyewitness accounts that made up the first descriptions reported within a few hours of the Rockne crash by newspapers and radio stations across the country. Those first recollections were raw, vivid, and in all probability, on-the-spot accurate.

"Looking up, the youth saw an airplane burst into flames and rocket toward the earth," the Sedalia (Mo.) Democrat reported Edward Baker's account published in the afternoon edition on March 31, 1931.

The Department of Commerce's lead investigator in Kansas City, Leonard Jurden, wasn't notified of the accident until 12:15 p.m. when newspapers called him to identify the plane. Jurden left Kansas City at about 2:30 p.m. and drove to the site with T&WA officials R.M. Jacobs, John Collins and R.S. Bridges. By the time Jurden arrived in Cottonwood Falls (where the bodies were taken) at about 7 p.m., souvenir scavengers were long gone after they had ravaged the crash site and taken off with significant chunks of the airliner that contained vital clues as to what may have caused the plane to come down.

The following day, that "explosion" was scaled down into second-day versions by witnesses who recounted hearing a "sputtering" engine that "backfired" in the clouds. Follow-up accounts reported no signs of fire, just a severed wing floating "like a feather" from the sky that landed separately from the rest of the wreckage. First-day details of a fiery plane spinning down from the sky washed out into second-day conjectures of ice forming on the wings.

Whether the Department of Commerce investigators coerced witnesses into backing off from their initial explosive descriptions can never be known. It was public knowledge that the Aeronautics Branch of the Department of Commerce, the federal government's regulating branch of air travel and the forerunner to the Federal Aviation Administration (FAA), had already spent five years fighting both press and public pressure to keep crash investigations confidential.

Herbert Hoover took charge of the Department of Commerce in 1926. The President quickly moved forward with the realization that commercial aviation would only prosper if the federal government managed the licensing of pilots and oversaw the safety of aircraft operation.

Hoover's policy infused quick progression into the commercial aviation industry under the leadership of two directors – William P. MacCracken and Col. Clarence Young. By 1930, 417,500 passengers were taking to the air, more than double the previous year's airline travel numbers of 173,300.

Commercial progress put the young industry under a public microscope. Since its inception under the Air Commerce Act of 1926, the Aeronautics Branch's policy of keeping findings of airplane crashes sealed brought relentless pressure from the national press. With more planes taking to the air, more accidents occurred – some due to manufacturing designs in experimental stages, others due to growing pains of an industry emerging from its infancy.

Every plane crash in the early days of aviation travel was a learning experience for a young Aeronautics Branch of the Department Commerce. Each crash presented a new set of circumstances for an agency crawling through its own infancy of conducting investigations.

Mounting pressure from the country's leading newspapers – The New York Times, Washington Daily News, Chicago Daily Tribune, and even the period's nationally renowned columnist Ernie Pyle – exerted First Amendment influence to force the Department of Commerce to make crash findings public. Pyle led the charge through his widely-read aviation column that appeared in syndication for the Scripps-Howard newspapers from 1928 to 1932.

The constant public push for transparency created a boiling pot of hostility between the press and the federal government. With more and more people choosing air travel, the general public demanded to know how safe passengers would be on a plane. The Department of Commerce's policy of keeping plane crash investigations secret began to succumb to the frequent demands of the country's watchdog press.

But the crash of T&WA Flight 5 was unprecedented. Not only was the crash the first high-profile airline tragedy to fall under the DOC's investigation jurisdiction, Rockne's death made it impossible for the Aeronautics Branch to conceal its findings in the cause. There had been a throng of airline crashes in previous years, but this one was special. If Knute Rockne could die in a plane crash, anyone could. The nation demanded answers. The Aeronautics Branch had no choice but to cave to the public's right to know and the media's right to publish for the sake of future aviation safety.

"The press, as well as people in all walks of life have looked toward the Dept. for an explanation of the catastrophy (sic)," DOC Aeronautics Branch officials acknowledged in an undated five-page statement that was included with the accident investigation's official report.

Faced with an airline crash that resulted in the death of a beloved American icon, the DOC had no choice but to break policy and go public. Filed April 15, 1931, the DOC report also cited an editorial from the New York Times.

"For the first time," the DOC stated, "the Department now makes public an air accident finding."

Still, reports of the Rockne crash needed to be tempered. An "explosion" in the air? The plane tumbled from the sky "in flames?" The last thing the federal government needed was public hysteria knocking down the doors of Washington over the possibility of a bomb being planted on the plane that killed the beloved Rockne.

16

ANTHONY FOKKER

The Flying Dutchman had nothing on the real Anthony Fokker.

Born Anton Herman Gerard "Anthony" Fokker on April 6, 1890, in the Dutch East Indies of what is now Indonesia, Anthony Fokker was 4 years old when his family returned to their native Netherlands to settle in Haarlem so Fokker and his older sister, Toos, could grow up with a traditional Dutch upbringing.

School was of little interest to Fokker. Yet, the Dutch teen who dropped out before he could complete high school possessed a keen natural sense for mechanics. Model trains and steam engines were his toys. Young Anthony loved nothing more than experimenting with designs of the earliest model airplanes.

In 1913, roughly around the same time Knute Rockne and Gus Dorais were perfecting their forward passing routes during summer workouts at Cedar Point in

Sandusky, Ohio, Fokker was 4,000 miles across the Atlantic Ocean perfecting a wheel that would not puncture. Although the idea had already been patented, it was Fokker who first installed a perimeter of a rubber wheel with a series of puncture-proof metal plates.

Fokker took a job as director of a Dutch manufacturing company. When World War I broke out, the German government moved in to take control of the factory. Staying on as the company's director and main design engineer, Fokker began designing aircraft for the Imperial German Army Air Service.

Among his most notable products included the Fokker Eindecker and the Fokker Dr. I, a triplane that gained instant worldwide fame for being the sophisticated war machine flown by German flying ace Manfred von Richtofen, famously known as the Red Baron. Fokker's company was responsible for delivering more than 700 military planes to the German air force, the German navy, and Austria and Hungary.

Fokker designed and manufactured the world's most renowned flying military bombers of the time period commanded by the likes of the Red Baron. He was also a skilled pilot who demonstrated his aircraft to Germany's highest-ranking leaders. Fokker worked closely with accomplished fighter pilot, Otto Parschau, to bring the Eindecker into military use. On one occasion both Fokker and Parschau demonstrated the aircraft, prompting flying ace Max Immelman to comment in a letter:

"Fokker, especially, amazed us with his skill."

Fokker's renown as an aviation pioneer who was equally skilled as a pilot on the same level as The Red Baron was immortalized in folklore. "The Flying Dutchman," a World War I flying ace based on Fokker who piloted the same skies with the Red Baron while cultivating his own magnanimous legend, was immortalized as the hero of films such as "Von Richthofen and Brown" and "Young Indiana Jones Chronicles: Attack of the Hawkmen."

When it came to business dealings, however, Fokker was a flawed man. His factory floor was filled with several prototypes in development and production at the same time, but he struggled to fulfill war contracts because he failed to reinvest his wartime profits. Fokker was not a formally educated engineer, which may have led to his distrust for qualified educated engineers and his resentment toward frequent German insistence that he conduct stringent structural tests to ensure that German-used aircraft were fit for combat.

Fokker's aloof disposition bordered on heartlessness. His nasty temper and insensitive disregard for a colleague's life flared up on June 27, 1916, when designer Martin Kreuzer crashed a prototype Fokker D.I. aircraft. As Kreuzer lay mortally injured gasping his last few breaths, Fokker proceeded to give a verbal report on the jammed rudder that caused the crash while wailing obscenities toward the dying pilot.

Fellow designer Reinhold Platz, who witnessed the incident, recounted later that Fokker "… hurried to the scene and shouted reproaches at the mortally injured man."

Fokker could also be charismatic with service pilots and charming to senior officers. His charm served him well when his newly delivered Fokker Dr.I triplanes suddenly began experiencing a string of fatal accidents in 1917. Still, that charm couldn't keep his Fokker Dr.I triplane from being temporarily grounded as too dangerous to fly.

The problem arose when the triplane's top wings ripped away under aerobatic conditions. In one instance, the Red Baron's brother, Lothar von Richthofen, miraculously survived a crash caused by a severed wing. Fokker proved to Germany's high command that the cause of the crashes was not due to the triplane's basic design, but the German military concluded that the plane's problems were due to shoddy workmanship under poor supervision and lax quality control at the Fokker factory.

Fokker received a stern warning, but the scenario repeated itself with the introduction of the E.V/D VIII monoplane in mid-1918. When a high-level German inquiry revealed more production and workmanship issues, German authorities threatened to file criminal charges against Fokker.

Instead of facing potential criminal charges, Fokker left Germany and returned to the Netherlands shortly after World War I came to an end. He blamed overzealous German Air Force inspectors for requiring what he considered to be an ill-conceived design change.

"When the first D-8 [sic] was submitted to the engineering division to be sand-load tested, the wings proved to be sufficiently strong, but the regulations called for a proportionate strength in the rear spar compared to the front spar," Fokker wrote in his responding report. "Complying with the government's edict, we strengthened the rear spar and started to produce in quantity..."

Fokker's troubles only mounted.

The D.VIII's wing continued to collapse at high speed. Fokker recalled the plane for further testing. After discovering that the reinforced rear spar caused the wings to flex unevenly at high speeds and increase the angle of attack at the wings' tips which caused the wing to shear apart under increased loads, Fokker resolved the problem by restoring the rear spar to his original specifications.

At the conclusion of World War I, the German Revolution swept through the Netherlands. Fokker escaped to the United States and immediately established the North American branch of his company, the Atlantic Aircraft Corporation, with facilities in New York and New Jersey. Upon arrival in the U.S., Fokker quickly began operations to develop the Fokker F-VII airplane.

Designed in 1924 by Walter Rethel as a single-engine transport aircraft, five aircrafts of the F.VII model were built for the Dutch airline KLM. One of the planes – the registered H-NACC – would be used in the first flight from the Netherlands to the Dutch East Indies. Lt. Commander Richard E. Byrd and Machinist Floyd Bennett also flew a Fokker F-VII during aviation history's first flight to the North Pole

In America, Fokker quickly became the world's largest aircraft manufacturer. The U.S. Army and Navy lined up to acquire his aircraft. Large carriers such as Pan American and TWA used Fokker's planes to transport passengers during the dawn of commercial aviation.

When word reached Fokker about the inaugural Ford Reliability Tour, proposed by the Ford Motor Company to develop competition for transport aircraft, Fokker instructed his company's head designer, Reinhold Platz, to convert a single-engine F.VII A airliner to a trimotor craft powered by 200-horsepower Wright Whirlwind radial engines.

The result, dubbed the Fokker F.VII A/3M, won the Ford Reliability Tour with a structure that consisted of a fabric-covered steel-tube fuselage and a plywood-skinned wooden wing. Fokker further modified the design into the Fokker F.VII B/3M with a slightly-increased wing area over the A/3M and a power increase to 220-horsepower per engine.

Out of the Fokker F.VII B/3M was born the Fokker F-10, a larger version of the B/3M built to carry 12 passengers in an enclosed cabin. The Fokker F-10, popularly known as the Fokker Trimotor, dominated the American market in the late 1920s and was the aircraft of choice for the world's largest airlines in Europe and the U.S.

More problems hit Fokker's American operations in 1927. Richard Byrd was planning to use a Fokker three-engine plane to be the first aviator to fly non-stop across the Atlantic Ocean, but the plane sustained damage during a test flight. Charles Lindbergh wound up flying the "Spirit of St. Louis," a single-engine monoplane designed by Donald A. Hall of Ryan Airlines, across the Atlantic for the first non-stop trans-Atlantic flight. That fatal test flight cost Fokker a place in aviation history books.

The Fokker aeronautics empire rebounded two years later when the "Question Mark," a modified Atlantic-Fokker C-2 transport plane used by the United States Army Air Corps commanded by Major Carl A. Spaatz, set new world records for flight endurance. During a non-stop flight that spanned 150 hours between January 1 and January 7, 1929, Fokker's Question Mark established world records for sustained flight, refueled flight, and distance before landing near Los Angeles, California.

Then, the Fokker F-10 Flight 599 crashed on March 31, 1931, killing Knute Rockne, five other passengers and both pilots. The aeronautics manufacturing empire Anthony Fokker had spent more than two decades building came to a grinding halt.

17

NON-GROUNDED

Three days prior to the crash, Anthony Fokker "personally inspected this plane" and signed off on the air ship's safety, DOC investigators stated in the Aeronautics Branch of the U.S. Department of Commerce's official accident investigation report.

Fokker's approval on his product's safety condition was business as usual. The Fokker F-10A Super Trimotor wooden-structured, wooden-winged aircraft operated with a payload of 12 passengers with three 425-horsepower Pratt & Whitney Wasp engines that could hit 154 miles an hour at top speed. Like all aircraft designed by the famous airship designer, the Fokker F-10A was said to be among the safest planes in the world during the late 1920s.

The military begged to differ.

Three months prior to the Rockne crash, the Fokker F-10 came under intense military scrutiny in the wake of extensive testing at Wright Field in Dayton, Ohio. U.S.

Army and Department of Commerce engineers revealed a suspect wooden wing structure that, when reaching a speed of 80 miles per hour, caused the plane to "fly like a duck."

"The plywood-covering checks in very good shape," wrote Dillard Hamilton, a National Parks Airways inspector, in a letter to Gilbert G. Budwig, director of air regulation for the Aeronautics Branch. "But I always worry about the spars and internal bracing. That is covered up where one cannot check."

Hamilton noted that a representative from Fokker's factory suggested adjusting the F-10's "allerons," or control surfaces on the wing, to "relieve tail heaviness." But Hamilton remained concerned that an adjustment – which entailed rigging the angle of alignment – might cause the pilot to lose control during a turn in bad weather.

Budwig replied: "We are not familiar with the factory recommendation... and do not believe that such rigging will correct tail heaviness. In view of the turning characteristics which you describe, it would be advisable to rig the allerons in the normal manner."

Further concerns arose when U.S. Navy officials summarily rejected the Fokker F-10A on two separate occasions during additional military testing in early 1931. The Navy's rejections prompted the Aeronautics Branch to announce intentions to ground the Fokker F-10A after Rear Admiral William A. Moffett, chief of the Navy Bureau of Aeronautics, made it known that a trial board ruled the F-10 "unstable" following a flight test at the Anacostia naval air station on January 15, 1931.

The Aeronautics Branch of the Department of Commerce took no immediate action. The Fokker F-10 remained in the air.

"Six passengers were manifested, only half filling the 12-place cabin..." retired U.S. Air Force Lt. Colonel Boardman C. Reed wrote in the January 1989 issue of "Vintage Airplane" magazine, "... but one had a change of plans at the last minute. Knute Rockne took his place."

Rockne was traveling on the overnight train to Kansas City when the Transcontinental Western Air Express Fokker F-10AF-1 NC 999E flew into Kansas City from Los Angeles. The plane was scheduled to be turned back to retrace its route to Los Angeles as "Flight 5" the next morning, March 31.

T&WA mechanic E.C. "Red" Long thought better of putting the plane in the air on his signature. Long had inspected the plane a few days before and found "... the wing panels were all loose on the wing. They were coming loose and it would take days to fix it, and I said the airplane wasn't fit to fly."

Long refused to sign the log. But an unknown T&WA supervisor pulled rank on the mechanic by claiming the company needed the plane in service.

"I don't know who signed the plane off, but they took the airplane," Long told DOC investigators. "Nobody was safe in that aircraft."

That morning, T&WA Flight 5 was supposed to depart Kansas City Municipal Airport at 8:30 a.m. The plane remained on the ground for 45 minutes to wait for a late shipment of mail. According to the investigation report, "...

the airline removed four seats from the rear of the plane and replaced it by a mail bin." The late-addition mail bin was filled with 28 pouches that weighed 95 pounds.

"Would that have any effect in balancing?" one investigator asked in the DOC official crash investigation report. "If Govt. or private inquiry shows that the airline was negligent, what penalty can the govt. inflict on the airline?"

T&WA employees would not have protested if Flight 5 had stayed grounded under mechanic Red Long's order. In the wake of drastic salary cuts outlined in the DOC investigation, pilots and mechanics were ready to walk off the job with morale among all employees "shot" after the company cut the pay of pilots "about 30%" with "no warning or notice," lead investigator Leonard Jurden wrote in a letter to Gilbert Budwig.

"Due to this condition and then the accident, morale sagged even lower and nerves ragged," Jurden noted.

Red flags all over Kansas City Municipal Airport that March 31, 1931 morning begged the question: Why was Fokker F-10A Flight 5 allowed to take off?

The T&WA flight mechanic had refused to sign off on the plane's structural safety. A last-minute ticket transfer had put Knute Rockne aboard as a passenger... meaning, the T&WA supervisor who overruled Red Long at the last minute knew that one of the most beloved sports figures in the country was potentially in danger of traveling on a plane that had already been determined by the military and T&WA to be structurally unsafe.

Takeoff was delayed for 45 minutes to await the arrival of a late mail shipment. Four passenger seats were removed to make space for a bin filled with 95 pounds of mail. Weather conditions were cold, cloudy and iffy. And T&WA employees were ready to walk off the job over sudden salary cuts.

Somebody wanted that plane carrying Knute Rockne in the air.

18

JOE-PETE

There wasn't a better pilot in 1931 to fly the Fokker F-10A Flight 5 under any conditions than Joe-Pete.

Master Sgt. Robert G. "Joe-Pete" Fry was a tall, 32-year-old former Marine fighter pilot who earned his wings in Guam in 1923 and was a fully designated Naval Aviation Pilot (NAP) by 1924. Over the next three years, Fry flew all over the United States from his station at Brown Field in Quantico, Virginia. In 1927, he was shipped out to China to fly with the 3rd Marine Expeditionary Force.

Joe-Pete's masterful knack for negotiating treacherous weather conditions in the sky was tested profoundly while flying Boeing FB-1 fighters with Fighting Squadron #10 out of Camp MacMurray at Hsin Ho, China in 1928.

Fry was flying a reconnaissance mission over hostile territory when he encountered a nasty major sand-wind storm and got lost. After skillfully maneuvering a miraculous forced landing safely to the ground, he suddenly found himself swarmed by Chinese rebels.

The Chinese suspected Joe-Pete to be a foreign spy, a captured prisoner of war who should be met with slow torture and a fatal bullet. But Joe-Pete not only carried masterful flight skills, he possessed an extraordinary wit that allowed him to keep calm under the most intense pressure. Using those wits, Joe-Pete convinced his captors that he was just a lost pilot with no interest in the Chinese Civil War.

The Chinese rebels bought the explanation. Fry was released back to the skies, and he returned safely to his base at Camp MacMurray.

Fry returned to the United States in April 1930. He was hired by Western Air Express with high Marine Corps' recommendations lauding his skills as "one of the ablest pilots produced from the enlisted ranks." With his China fighter-pilot pal Harlan Hull, who was also hired by Western Air Express, Fry remained in the Marine Corps Reserves while flying for Western Air Express – which would later merge with Transcontinental to form Transcontinental & Western Air (T&WA).

Fry settled into a daily route flying a regular schedule between Kansas City and Los Angeles that allowed him to maintain residences in both cities. Before flying on March 31, 1931, Joe-Pete had logged an impressive total of 1,263 hours and 33 minutes as a pilot, plus 227 hours and 57 minutes as a co-pilot. His co-pilot, Herman J. Mathias, also had 219 hours and 23 minutes under his belt. Over the previous 90 days Fry had logged 191 hours and 36 minutes, flying 2,511 of those miles at night. Mathias' previous 90-day log showed 112 hours and 29 minutes.

Fry flew the Fokker F-10A plane to Los Angeles from Kansas City on March 30. He departed routinely at the regularly scheduled 8:15 a.m. takeoff time, and returned to Kansas City without incident to repeat the flight on March 31.

Although probable, it was never documented whether Fry knew the plane had been grounded by Red Long before it was cleared for flight. With the takeoff time delayed waiting for a late mail shipment, Fry kept his eye on the weather reports. Kansas City skies were overcast with very light snow falling at times and mild winds from the north at two-to-three miles per hour. Fry figured he would catch clear weather over Salina by about 10:15 a.m. Wichita - the first stop - reported clear, hazy weather with temperatures at 37 degrees and winds out of the northwest at 10 miles per hour.

Bad weather didn't concern Joe-Pete in the least. He'd flown through bad weather on countless occasions. If he could navigate through a nasty, windy sandstorm over China and negotiate a landing that few, if any, on the planet could have survived, he could get the plane from Kansas City to Los Angeles.

Bad weather was nothing new to Joe-Pete, just part of the job. T&WA's most skilled pilot was much more concerned about having his pay cut by 30 percent.

19

IN FLIGHT

At 9:15 a.m., Transcontinental & Western Air Flight 5 departed Kansas City Municipal Airport following a 45-minute delay. On board, according to the flight's log, were Knute Rockne and five other passengers.

T&WA operations supervisor Jack Frye watched Robert Fry expertly navigate a smooth 600-yard crosswind takeoff until the dark red and silver Fokker F-10AF-1 NC-999E disappeared above the low-lying ceiling of clouds.

Fifteen minutes after Flight 5 departed, Paul E. Johnson, an airmail pilot flying for National Air Transport, took off from the same runway in Kansas City and headed towards Coffeeville, Arkansas. Johnson flew on "good weather reports given," despite Kansas City weather that showed a 500-foot cloud ceiling.

"Had to go up the Missouri River and out through the valley south of the Kaw River, and continuous north of regular course down Emporia because of the weather conditions," Johnson wrote in his flight report contained in the Aeronautics Branch's investigation report.

"Low ceiling and misty rain between Kansas City and Emporia, with alternate icy pick-ups and holes with good weather for four or five miles," Johnson noted. "Took... 40 minutes to get to Emporia, where... ran into low drifts of fog, snow-covered ground, and had to fly under drifts. Ran into wall of fog west of Emporia about 10 miles and started to turn towards the northwest where the weather appeared to be clearing. Started to pick up ice very rapidly and was flying just over the tree tops. Afraid to turn around and come back to Kansas City because of the Fokker, which I assumed to be in the rear of my ship."

At 9:52 a.m., a cold front knifed into a warming zone over the red Flint Hills. Fry was in radio contact with Kansas City flying 10 miles southwest of Ottawa, 40 minutes out of Kansas City, when the weather suddenly grew heavier.

T&WA radio operator G.A. O'Reily in Wichita contacted Flight 5 to get an update.

"I can't talk now, too busy," Co-pilot Herman J. Mathias responded.

"What are you going to do?" O'Reily asked.

"I don't know," Mathias replied.

At 10:22, flying 25 miles northeast of Cassoday, Kansas, the NAT plane flew close enough to the Fokker F-10 for the pilots to wave at each other. Johnson overtook and passed above Flight 5. The Fokker Trimotor may have been capable of a top-end speed of 154 mph, but the plane drudged slowly at its optimum maneuvering speed of 102-103 mph, well below its 126 mph cruising capabilities.

"I then turned northwest after the second drift, intending to turn around to the right," Johnson told investigators later. "That was the last time I saw the F-10. It was turning, too, to the northwest."

Mathias radioed the T&WA station in Wichita: Flight 5 was on course 35 miles north of the Cassoday beacon light near Emporia.

O'Reily responded: "The sun is shining in Wichita."

Mathias' voice came back muddy through static: "The weather is getting tough. We've been forced too low by clouds. We're going to turn around and go back to Kansas City."

A few minutes later, Mathias radioed back: Flight 5 is going to try once more to get through the bad weather. The co-pilot told O'Reily to stand by.

Mrs. E.S. Chartier, a weather observer in Emporia, Kansas, reported general weather conditions as "improved quite an extent" from an earlier forecast. The cloud ceiling had risen, first to 1,200 feet, then to 1,500 feet. A higher ceiling was expected by noon.

At 10:40 a.m., Mrs. Chartier broadcast a "peculiar depressing condition" in the air, a "cyclonic atmosphere," a dark funnel-shaped cloud in the southwest.

The NAT plane headed west and started climbing in altitude. At 800 feet the plane encountered a 50-foot space between fog and low clouds. Johnson turned the plane south, then southwest toward Cassoday where good weather was being reported. Johnson's plane picked up ice very rapidly. No way it could fly higher than 1,500 feet.

"Ice on struts, allerons bowed," Johnson reported. "Air speed indicator iced up." Johnson flew relying on the turn indicator, climb indicator and tachometer. Ice was too heavy for the plane to gain more altitude. The NAT plane's motor flew wide open until Johnson "broke out of everything 15 miles straight east of Wichita."

Johnson landed the NAT plane safely in Wichita.

At 10:45, Fry and Mathias were unable to radio their position. In Wichita, O'Reily radioed weather conditions: "Practically clear and unlimited visibility seven miles, wind northwest... few clouds northeast."

"We've headed back but it's getting tighter," Mathias said. "Think we'll come on to Wichita, it looks pretty bad."

"Can you get through? O'Reily asked.

There was no response. O'Reily repeated his question.

"Don't know yet. Don't know yet," Mathias replied.

Those were the last words Wichita air traffic control received from Transcontinental & Western Air Flight 5.

20

A CORONER'S JURY

Leonard Jurden, TWA district agent H.G. Edgerton of Wichita, T&WA President Harris Hanshue, and Anthony Fokker were among the first investigative authorities called to analyze the carnage and determine the cause of the crash.

Their first stop was Cottonwood Falls, where the bodies of Rockne and the seven other victims had been taken. By the time they arrived on the scene, much of the plane – large pieces of wing, fuselage, and other significant parts that might have revealed the actual cause of the crash – had been snatched up by souvenir hunters and hauled away.

"Department investigators learned from eyewitnesses that the airplane was flying at an altitude between 500-600 feet apparently in a northeast direction, the assumption being that the pilot turned north of his course to avoid an unfavorable weather condition," Jurden wrote in the investigation report.

Two days after the crash, a coroner's jury convened in Cottonwood Falls to hear testimony by farmers who witnessed the catastrophe. Professional aviation experts were also called in to offer circumstantial theories in an effort to determine the cause.

Four farmers testified at the coroner's jury – Edward Baker; his brother, Arthur Baker; R.C. Blackburn; and Clarence H. McCracken. All gave similar eyewitness accounts. Edward Baker's statement in the accident investigation report coincided with his brother's account, but his recollection two days later slightly varied from the "terrific explosion" he heard in the clouds that was recounted to newspaper reporters at the scene of the crash.

Edward Baker explained to DOC investigators that he and his brother, Arthur, were about one and one-half miles away from the scene when they heard a plane in the clouds twice – five minutes apart. The first plane was likely the NAT plane piloted by Paul Johnson. The second time, Edward Baker said, the plane sounded as if the pilot had gunned the motor and shut it off with some backfire – and then the crash happened. Edward Baker told Jurden he saw only the wing fall, "... but not the main part of the plane."

McCracken recalled feeding cattle on Steward Baker's farm at the time. "The engine sounded all right until it was falling," he said. The plane emerged from the clouds "very fast," almost straight down. McCracken maintained that when the plane came out of the clouds, one motor seemed to be sputtering. A hill obscured McCracken's view of the plane hitting the ground.

"A few seconds after the ship came out of the clouds, I saw part of the wing come down, drifting slowly," McCracken said. "When the ship came out of the clouds it seemed to me to be going end over end. After the plane hit and (the) wing came down, there were objects that came floating down."

"I heard the plane flying above the clouds, hanging low over the ground," R.C. Blackburn testified. "The motor was sputtering... Suddenly the plane shot out of the clouds, it was tipping to one side and headed straight for the earth. A moment later I saw part of the wing floating down."

"It might have been backfiring, then we heard a sound which may have been the crash," Edward Baker said. "I said the plane must have exploded. Just after the plane fell, we saw the wing come down."

Blackburn remembered arriving at the site and scouring the wreckage. The break in the wing "appeared a little ragged and splintered, but went square across. An unbroken light on the top side, number side up." He also spotted a bag of mail under the wing and "three more sacks" between the wing and the plane.

L.E. Mann told the jury he rode to the site with Wallace Evans, Blackburn, and three others, including Dr. A.E. Titus. All helped remove the bodies. Mann said an hour had passed before he was able to get a good look at the wing. "U-shaped pieces of ice lying around the wing, about 6 inches long," he recounted.

Anthony Fokker flew over the scene on April 2nd with Jack Frye, TWA's operations supervisor. He picked up a small piece of the wing left behind and part of the bottom flange of the spar, "which showed a break under tension...

"Material and glue joints, all perfect," Fokker insisted. He pointed out that he had analyzed some middle pieces of the spar directly above the fuselage, and a part of the wing that had been brought back to the spot where the plane had crashed.

Fokker concluded that the break was not caused by propeller failure, which countered DOC investigators' original findings. The right engine, Fokker said, struck the ground first, showing that the plane fell sideways and backwards. He suggested that the plane crashed at an "excessive speed" following a prolonged dive. Figuring the pilot lost control temporarily, or that everyone "was thrown forward including luggage and mail... If the luggage and mail sacks in the compartment were not properly secured or strapped down, a shifting load might fall forward into the pilot's cockpit, crash through roof or windows, or fall forward on the steering column, causing it to jam and (the) pilot unable to recover."

Otherwise, the plane's designer theorized that "... pilot may have lost control on account of inexperience in blind flying, through failure or faulty indication of navigation instruments, or through excessive ice formation on the airplane."

Four pilots gave their own expert opinions to Aeronautics Branch investigator Fred H. Grieme. Each theoretically agreed with Fokker that weather caused Fry to lose control of the plane. Each also shared the theory that Fry appeared to get caught in bad weather, tried to pull through it, and fell into a spin resulting in losing the wing.

But one co-pilot knew Fry too well to agree with the four theorists. The co-pilot, only documented by his last name, "Herford," had flown with Fry on several occasions. He steadfastly insisted that Fry was not to blame. "He was considered as one of the best blind flyers in the (T&WA) company, and he always pulled through the fogs and clouds on leaving (Los Angeles)," Herford maintained.

Grieme wrote in the DOC accident investigation report that "Co-pilot Herford... did not think Fry would get into trouble flying blind and was sure that something unusual had happened."

21

OFFICIAL INCONCLUSIONS

Investigators initially determined that weather moisture

was a factor after finding that the plane's plywood outer skin was bonded to the ribs and spars with water-based aliphatic resin glue. Flying through rain caused the bond to deteriorate, causing sections of the plywood to suddenly separate in flight and sever the wing.

That was one theory.

The Department of Commerce issued a release blaming the crash on a broken propeller on the right engine. Ice, the investigators surmised, had formed on the propeller hub, which may have broken loose and struck one of the propeller blades. The propeller blade broke, created an unbalanced condition, and produced sufficient vibration to cause not only the hub and remaining blades to leave the engine, but also accounted for the in-flight wing separation... this analysis was determined after investigators dug the engine out of the ground, but couldn't find the engine's propeller hub or blades.

On April 8, the Department of Commerce issued a second press release that contradicted the first.

The cause of the crash was not due to broken propeller, the second release stated. The propeller and the hub were eventually located "...underground beneath the place where the engine, to which it had been attached, was dug out of the earth."

Investigators constructed a new theory: Ice formed on the aircraft and rendered the pilot's instruments inoperative while flying in the clouds, which caused the pilot to become disoriented and the aircraft to spiral into a deep dive. When the pilot reoriented himself, he overstressed the wing by trying to correct the unusual aircraft altitude too rapidly, which caused the wing to separate.

The Department of Commerce's revised theory appeared to be little more than conjecture put out by investigators who didn't really know what caused the crash but were desperate to toss theories against the wall to see which one stuck. Newspaper columnist Ernie Pyle blasted the investigation for looking more like a federal goose chase conducted by incompetents who were chasing their own tail.

"Do you know the old expression, 'eating crow?'" Pyle wrote in his syndicated column on April 8. "Well, the Department of Commerce is eating crow today on the Rockne crash. And since I was thoroughly sold on the

Department's original explanation of the accident, I have ordered a nice plateful of crow for my own lunch."

The New York Times cut deeper into the Department of Commerce's haphazard findings. The Times slammed the DOC for rushing to judgment to appease a public left just as confused by the investigation's second official conclusion as the first.

"This was the first time the Commerce Department had made public the findings of its inspectors," the Times editorialized on April 8. "Officials indicated the reversal of policy was prompted by the tremendous public interest aroused by the sudden death of one of the greatest football figures in history."

Blackburn and the Bakers agreed there was no ice on the plane. Department of Commerce inspector Leonard Jurden testified to pilot Robert Fry, a former U.S. Marine Corps pilot with 4,500 hours of flight experience under his belt, as being "wholly competent." Jack Frye, vice president of T&WA operations, admitted to the jury that he couldn't make a determination until he had conducted a further investigation. T&WA field manager A.L. Sondine said the plane had been inspected twice and "reported in good condition" on two occasions immediately preceding the fatal crash.

Passengers on the plane weighed in at a combined 915 pounds. Baggage added 146 pounds. There was a discrepancy in the weight of the mail, originally listed at 63.6 pounds but raised to nearly 95 pounds after the late shipment arrived.

Mail sacks were found on the ground between the broken wing and the main fuselage. Two more bags were found 50 yards away in the southeast direction of where the broken wing lay. The smallest sack – labeled from Kansas City to Wichita – was retrieved from underneath the broken wing when investigators lifted about an 18-foot section of the wing, indicating that wing failure occurred near stations 8-11 where the engine attachment points were located on the one-piece wooden wing.

Edward Baker testified, "… a good-sized piece of wood came down after the wing, a little south and east of the main plane."

Was that piece a lighter piece of the wing, perhaps blown higher into the air by an explosion?

Fokker stood by his initial determination, "...the human element.

"In my opinion. The ship was placed in a violent maneuver and the wing was torn off as a result... Three hundred ships like the one which crashed have been built in conformity with the same design. There has been no accident of major importance to them where the cause appeared to be a structural failure of a wing."

But the words of Fry's former co-pilot, Herford, overwhelmed the others' hypothetical criticisms of Joe-Pete Fry's flying skills. Herford's contention that Fry "...was considered as one of the best blind flyers in the company, and he always pulled through the fogs and clouds on leaving (Los Angeles)," spoke the loudest.

Grieme noted in the DOC report that "Co-pilot Herford... did not think Fry would get into trouble flying blind and was sure that something unusual had happened."

The coroner's jury found the cause of the crash to be "undetermined."

The Department of Commerce's official findings were also "inconclusive."

22

UNCENSORED!

Something unusual did happen, according to a booklet published less than two months after the crash.

"UNCENSORED! TRUTH ABOUT ROCKNE'S STRANGE DEATH... Not a Broken Propeller, Not Ice on the Wing... At Last - Inside Story of the Fatal Crash" immediately raised questions over the likely possibility that the plane carrying Knute Rockne was sabotaged. "UNCENSORED! shredded the Department of Commerce's findings as nothing more than hypothetical "conjecture."

The book, published by Graphics Arts, Corporation in Minneapolis, Minnesota, is a collector's item today.

"Considering the purpose of the investigation and the frequent lack of direct information, investigators have been obliged to draw on their flying knowledge and experience to set up certain assumptions in arriving at conclusions with reference to this particular accident," "UNCENSORED!"

claimed. "Therefore, the assignment of causes as shown are to a substantial extent premised upon opinion and conjecture."

In addition to printing investigators' official findings, "UNCENSORED!" delved deeply into coverage of specifics of the Fokker Trimotor plane and details of the pilots' final radio communications with air traffic controllers at Wichita Airport. The book also addressed contradictions between newspaper and eyewitness accounts.

"None have yet dared to tell the truth about the horrible tragedy that destroyed the greatest and most beloved man in the history of American sport," the book's authors claimed. "Has the truth been suppressed for selfish and cowardly reasons?"

The writers cited airline officials' conclusions that the Fokker Trimotor plane carrying Rockne was less than two years old and in nearly new mechanical condition with a "comparatively small number of flying hours chalked against it."

"In conclusion," the book contended, "it would seem that the airplane involved had been operated entirely in accordance with the Air Commerce Regulations; that the daily inspections were satisfactorily concluded; that the airplane was, to the best of everyone's knowledge, thoroughly airworthy; and also, that no blame can be attached to the pilots."

"UNCENSORED!" also reveals, "Digging deep into the ground, the missing propeller blades were found!"

Finding the propellers and the split hub cap buried under the debris lent credence to the theory that the pilot, in his futile attempts to pull the plane out of a steep dive without the benefit of certain flight instruments rendered inoperative due to ice collected on the plane's outer shell, had "wrenched away the wing."

But Aeronautics Branch investigators found no traces of ice on the plane. Fokker, himself, admitted that of all of his 300 planes of the same type, none ever experienced an accident caused by a wing that failed. Fokker's wings were noted for tremendous durability, built to withstand loads 11 times greater than a load imposed on a wing under flying conditions detailed in the DOC's findings.

Pilot Robert Fry's flight skills were also regarded as tops among his peers at the time. Veteran fliers, including Army and transport pilots, went public refusing to believe that an experienced pilot of Fry's caliber would go into a nose dive and rip off a wing. Besides, they reasoned, eyewitnesses said the plane had been flying low under the clouds, not high enough for the plane to go into a nose dive.

Considering the supreme condition of the plane, and considering the plane's low-flying altitude seen moments before the crash, a clue to the actual cause of the crash may have been implied in an artist's rendering published in "CENSORED!" The sketch shows the left wing breaking off in the air and falling to the ground before landing about a half-mile from the bulk of the wreckage.

What could cause the wing to sever?

"Some of the theories advanced that the wing gave way of its own accord or because of an unusual load are ridiculous," said one Army air service pilot quoted in "UNCENSORED!" "But it's not ridiculous to consider that time after time we have had examples of sabotage, and that this might have happened to the Rockne plane, for reasons unknown."

The pilot described acts of sabotage he had seen on various aircraft. A mechanic working on a giant dirigible at Goodrich had been caught spitting on points where rivets were fastened to the framework knowing that the rivets would loosen - after they had passed inspection. Had the mechanic's acts not been discovered, "...the dirigible would have been wrecked on its first voyage," the pilot said.

"Airplanes in the Army and Navy have been tampered with to our definite knowledge, not once but many times," the pilot admitted. "Case after case is on the records" of gas lines sawed through, struts weakened, and other parts such as cotter pins removed from tail controls - all so parts would break and cause a plane to crash in what would seemingly appear to be a tragic accident.

"A bolt sawed half through, then covered with black gum; a hidden wire nicked with pliers - all those things are possible," the pilot insisted.

"UNCENSORED!" failed to mention eyewitness Edward Baker by name. But the book clearly confirmed the teen farmer's account of hearing what sounded like a bomb exploding on the plane in midair, a confirmation that was further magnified two years later in shocking headlines first printed by the South Bend News-Times in January 1933.

According to the South Bend News-Times, an "unimpeachable source" revealed that the United States

Secret Service had investigated the possibility of a bomb planted on the plane - a bomb that may have been intended for a Notre Dame priest, Father John Reynolds, set by Al Capone's gang after Father Reynolds testified in the murder trial of Capone henchman Leo Brothers. The source also maintained that Secret Service knew the identification of the mobster who planted the bomb in a mail pouch, but didn't reveal the name.

Two months after the South Bend News-Times story exposed the Rockne crash as a possible gangland bombing, the "City of Liverpool" - an Armstrong-Whitworth Argosy II passenger plane put out by the British airline Imperial Airways - crashed near the Belgium city of Diksmuide. The deadliest crash in British civil aviation history at the time killed all 15 people on board.

Or did it?

Witnesses on the ground in northern Belgium saw the plane burst into flames in the sky before it lost altitude and plunged to the ground. Those same onlookers watched one passenger jump out of the aircraft without a parachute and free-fall to the Earth.

Crash investigators later identified the remains of the exiting passenger as Dr. Albert Voss, a German national who had worked as a dentist in the United Kingdom. Their investigation found that a fire had started in either the lavatory or the luggage area in the rear of the plane's cabin, possibly ignited by either a combustible substance lit accidentally by a passenger, crew member, or the natural occurrence of a vibration.

During the inquest into Dr. Voss's death, his estranged brother came forward and told jurors that the dentist and his niece had been on the flight together completely aware that they were under investigation by Scotland Yard for drug smuggling. Dr. Voss, according to his brother, had used the airlines to travel around Europe and buy anesthetics he sold on the side that provided a lucrative income in addition to his dental practice.

Prior to the flight, the brother noted, Dr. Voss had purchased airline accident insurance. He had planned to escape his pursuers by destroying the plane with incendiary materials available to him through his dental practice then bailing out in the pandemonium with all intentions of surviving. But an inquest into Voss's death showed that, other than a few minor burns, Voss's body – unlike the other 14 victims whose remains were retrieved mangled beyond recognition - had otherwise been unharmed before he had exited the plane.

The inquest jury returned an "open verdict." Jurors concluded that while they believed Dr. Voss's death may not have been accidental, they didn't have concrete evidence to reach a definite decision. The brother's testimony, however, caused many to view the crash of the "City of Liverpool" as the first act of sabotage in commercial airline history.

Seven months later on Oct. 10, 1933, the fatal crash of a Boeing 247 airplane near Chesterton, Indiana hit too close to home to the Rockne crash for any bomb theorists to ignore.

United Airlines Flight 23 took off from Newark, New Jersey headed on a cross-country route toward Oakland, California with a first scheduled stop in Cleveland. With four passengers and three crew members aboard, the aircraft was on its way to its next stop in Chicago shortly after 9 p.m. when it exploded at an altitude of about 1,000 feet in mid-air.

Eyewitnesses on the ground heard the explosion and saw the plane plunge to the ground in flames. The plane exploded a second time on impact in a wooded area on the Jackson Township farm of landowner James Smiley. All four passengers and three crew members perished, including Alice Scribner, the first flight attendant in United Airlines history to be killed in a plane crash.

Findings from the debris left crash investigators stunned. The plane's toilet and baggage compartment had been obliterated into fragments. Metal shards pierced the inside of the toilet door only; the outside was completely devoid of metal traces. The plane's tail section had completely severed from the fuselage and was found a mile away, still intact.

Dr. Carl Davis from the Porter County Coroner's office and investigators from the Crime Detection Laboratory at Northwestern University collectively concluded that the crash of United Airlines aircraft NC 13304 had been caused by a nitroglycerin-fueled bomb. Famed federal agent Melvin Purvis, who at the time headed the Chicago office of the United States Bureau of Investigation, offered a poignant description of the probe's result.

"Our investigation convinced me that the tragedy resulted from an explosion somewhere in the region of the baggage compartment in the rear of the aircraft," Purvis said. "Everything in front of the compartment was blown forward, everything behind blown backward, and things at the side outward... The gasoline tanks, instead of being blown out, were crushed in, showing there was no explosion in them."

A further look into the cause revealed that a packaged rifle had been retrieved from the wreckage. Investigators dismissed the gun as evidence when they learned the weapon had been carried aboard as baggage for a passenger returning home to Chicago from New York to attend an event at Chicago's North Shore Gun Club. With limited remains available after local souvenir hunters arrived at the crash site and made off with significant plane parts, investigators were certain that the cause was a bomb.

Why?

Some considered the possibility of a bomb being planted to hurt United Airlines in a labor dispute, but the company had a stellar reputation for working well with unions and its employees. The destination, Chicago, was rife with Mafia activity. Purvis, however, failed to develop any leads that implicated any mob links to the crash.

A motive for the bombing of United Flight 23 remained a mystery even after an elderly man named Howard Johnson – who had driven to the wreck site in his Ford Model T - came forward 66 years later and recounted something he had heard during an oral history project organized by the Westchester Public Library in northwest Indiana.

"It was all rather vague, but they said that someone got on the plane in Cleveland and had a suitcase and then they got off and no one saw them take the suitcase off," Johnson recalled in 1999. "So that's, no doubt, what happened. They just left the bomb on the plane."

The bombing of Flight 23 was said to be the first proven case of air sabotage in the history of commercial aviation. Considering the circumstances surrounding the Diksmuide crash a few months earlier, the incident over Chesterton, Indiana may have actually been the second known airliner bombing.

Then there was the Rockne crash two years earlier that shared several similarities: Witnesses claimed to have heard an explosion in the air. The tail was severed from the fuselage on Flight 23 and found on the ground about a mile away nearly intact; the wing that had separated from the fuselage on the Fokker F-10 was recovered more than a half-mile away from the Kansas wreckage site completely intact. In both cases, souvenir hunters made off with substantial pieces from the respective wreckages before investigators could arrive and collect significant plane parts that may have held key details regarding a definitive cause… or, a saboteur.

The two proven cases that occurred within months of each other two years later fuel the possibility that the crash of the Fokker F-10 that killed Knute Rockne and seven others on March 31, 1931 may have actually been the first act of commercial airliner sabotage in United States aviation history.

23

GOD'S HANDFUL

Whatever dying words Jake Lingle whispered into the ear of the priest who cradled his last breath remained secret forever.

Father John Reynolds survived on his own terms. He wore the burden of his Bible-sworn testimony that created the untimely death of his beloved friend under his collar. Tell the truth. The whole truth. And nothing but the truth. Leave the consequences to God.

And always stay true to the sacramental seal of confessional.

A Chicago gangster might have put it this way: Never snitch on the confessor. Jake Lingle rests in eternal peace knowing that his dying words never passed Father Reynolds' mortal lips.

The rest of the story followed Father Reynolds like an extraordinary aura for the rest of his life. There was no sacramental seal to keep him from talking about the events that led to the crash that killed his friend Rockne to anyone who wished to listen. The truth may have been lost in the priest's brash nature, but it was Father Reynolds' fixed truth every time no matter how many years had piled up behind him.

"Yeah he did," said Father Richard Layton, a resident priest since 1969 at Our Lady of Guadalupe Abbey in Lafayette, Oregon, where Father Reynolds spent the final 24 years of his life. "The message I got was that he saw it, and he went over to the dying man... and supposedly heard his confession. He always believed that they were out to catch him, because he might have information through the confession. And then he just had an idea that somehow this was involved with (Knute Rockne) being killed in the plane accident.

"We didn't know whether to take it with a grain of salt or whatever, but he would tell the same story, pretty much in the same details. So, either he may have had an overactive imagination, but apparently most of the facts are there as far as his being there and the confession, and feeling rather unsafe."

Father Reynolds left Notre Dame in 1939. After entering the Holy Cross Order and joining the Trappists, a Catholic order of contemplative monks, he traveled to Kentucky in 1944, where he took residence at the Trappist Abbey Gethsemani and worked as a professor alongside noted writer Thomas Merton. The strong heads of Merton and Father Reynolds locked horns on more than one occasion during Father Reynolds' short stay at Gethsemani.

"Remote... he was a poet," is how Father Reynolds described Merton, who had been accepted into the monastery as a postulant by Gethsemani's Abbot, Frederic Dunne, and spent his time at Gethsemani writing journals and studying the complicated Cistercian sign language along with his daily work and worship routines.

"He tried to highbrow me, see, and I highbrowed him and he couldn't take it," Father Reynolds recalled of his relationship with the writer. "One time I was going through a door and he looked at me and he gritted his teeth at me. I looked at him and walked by."

Within a few months, Father Reynolds was shipped out of Gethsemani and sent west to Huntsville, Utah, to set up the Trappist Abbey of Our Lady of the Holy Trinity. His devotion to the priesthood was never questioned at Our Lady of the Holy Trinity, where he served as a one-man theological and philosophical faculty at the Trappist Abbey for the first four years.

"In those days," Father Reynolds remembered, "life was rugged and corn flakes frequent."

And Johnnie Reynolds remained a handful.

Father Reynolds never shed that angry little boy with the hair-trigger temper who grew up punching noses at the drop of a hat. Nor did Father Reynolds seem to care about putting the soul of Johnnie Reynolds behind him, a head-strong stubbornness that landed the holy man in several fights with fellow priests and monks over the years.

The last straw in Utah occurred in 1962. After 18 years, the spiritual and administrative leader of the Trappist

Abbey of Our Lady of the Holy Trinity had had enough of Johnnie Reynolds.

"He literally got thrown out of that monastery," Father Layton recalled. "He was a feisty little guy, 5-foot-6, maybe 5-foot-5, he was very feisty. The story goes that when he was at Holy Trinity, he got into a fight with one of the other brothers... he got the guy in a half-nelson, in one of those knuckle sandwiches. That was enough: The abbot said, 'You gotta go.'

"So, we took him in here."

In 1962, Father Reynolds settled for the rest of his life at Our Lady of Guadalupe Abbey in Lafayette, Oregon. He converted to the Order of Cistercians of the Strict Observance and changed his name to Father Simon. Johnnie Reynolds, however, stayed the same talkative, joyously argumentative, cantankerous spirit that refused to leave his embattled youth in Bellows Falls.

"Everybody's hair shirt," is how one fellow Our Lady of Guadalupe monk described Father Reynolds.

"You want me to call him a curmudgeon?" Father Layton asked through a chuckle.

"One of the things he used to do, if you coughed in chapel, or if you were in choir and you coughed, he would cough back. I think he had an issue about sounds; certain sounds made him angry. So, if there was a guest in the guest chapel coughing, he would look out there and maybe cough back. He was a feisty little guy. He was in track... he was very athletic in his younger years, so, he liked to pick a fight.

"One time," Father Layton recollected, "our Brother Fabian got after him because he was doing this - coughing after you cough - and he grabbed Father Simon and said, 'Stop that.'

"Simon said, 'You're gonna be excommunicated because you touched a priest.'"

Growing old while living among the wine vineyards of Oregon's serene wilderness mellowed Father Simon profoundly. He became accepted as the monastery's most "colorful" monk, and on June 16, 1982, his fellow monks at Guadalupe helped him celebrate the 60th anniversary of his ordination into the priesthood.

"He made it well here at Guadalupe," Father Layton said. "Because, any other place, they would've thrown him out, probably.

"But you know, in his last three months of life, he was dying. He turned extremely gentle, very gentle. We had a good time together. He was very nice, too. He had a soft spot, but he had that feisty attitude. Those three months before he died, those three months were very peaceful. I think death was on its way."

Father Simon's beard served as a form of personal restitution. Brother Fabian, Father Simon's chief antagonist at Guadalupe, wore a beard. Father Layton believed Father Simon grew his beard – a long, thick, bushy mass of hair that covered his face just like Brother Fabian's – as an act of contrition.

"I always felt he was doing that in reparation," Father Layton said. "He would make up for things. He was the kind of guy; he would make amends by doing something to show that he had made a mistake. I think those last days he knew that the end was coming, and he just gave up the fight."

At the turn of 1986, Ron Karten, a reporter from Catholic Sentinel newspaper in Portland, Oregon, traveled to Our Lady of Guadalupe Abbey to interview Father Reynolds about his extraordinary life. When Karten arrived, he found a "very small, very old," Trappist monk wearing a black hooded robe, black-rimmed glasses, a long thick white beard, and a warm smile that greeted the writer with open arms.

Karten recorded the interview on a series of cassette tapes. The 91-year-old monk impressed Karten with a sharp mind, keen intellect, and a clear memory that recalled specific details of his life as if they had happened that morning.

"One of the most intelligent men I've ever encountered," Karten recalled.

It didn't take long for the interview to turn to that June 1930 day in Chicago when Father Reynolds witnessed the murder of Jake Lingle. During the interview, Father Reynolds recounted testifying at trial that Brothers "looked like" Lingle's killer, but refused to say outright that Brothers actually pulled the trigger. He made no mention of Lingle's dying confession, and he referred to Frankie Foster as "Frank Shepperd," one of the gangster's several aliases.

The conversation landed on the crash that killed Rockne. Father Reynolds didn't flinch from the same account he gave 52 years before to the two students hanging out in his rector's office at St. Edwards Hall - James Bacon and Kitty Gorman.

He was old, kinder, gentler, mellow as a lamb in the final weeks of his life, but Father Reynolds still held Johnnie Reynolds in his soul - the tough priest from Bellows Falls who once came face to face on the street with the real killer of Jake Lingle and his six mob goons. As he did that day outside the train station in Chicago, Father Reynolds chuckled out loud at the recollection of the notorious mobsters looking like children as they piled back into their car.

"I never feared death from those men," Father Reynolds maintained, "because you only die once, and you don't die until God calls you."

"Now, what happened with the plane?" Karten inquired.

"To the plane?" the priest asked. "They bombed it."

"That Rockne was on?"

"Yeah," Father Reynolds replied.

"Were you supposed to be on that plane?"

"No, no," he said. "It was going out to make a picture, see... But all of the newspaper headquarters were phoning me wanting to know if I was on the plane, see, and I told them I wasn't.

"But," Father Reynolds insisted, "that is the way they got even with Notre Dame."

"The mob rubbed out Knute Rockne because they let you testify?"

"Yeah, yup, absolutely, oh I am sure of that...oh, yeah..."

Father Reynolds paused.

"Isn't that some story?" he asked with a grin. "You like that story? I have plenty more."

His last night on Earth, Father Simon Reynolds penned a cryptic note that wound up pinned to the Our Lady of Guadalupe community bulletin board.

"Everybody is invited to my homecoming," the note read.

But Johnnie Reynolds wasn't about to go out without delivering one last act of defiance.

"We asked if he wanted to make Guadalupe his monastery of stability, but he refused," Father Layton said. "He wanted to remain as a monk of Holy Trinity, but some of that was in spite of the Abbot at that time, the Abbot of Holy Trinity. (Father Reynolds) would always insist that he was still a monk at Holy Trinity.

"At the end, the Abbot (at Guadalupe) asked if he wanted to be buried here, and he said, 'Yes,' so he kind of let go a lot of those grudges and resentments."

On the morning of January 28, 1986, Trappist Father John Simon Reynolds died at the age of 91. Later that day, the space shuttle Challenger exploded in mid-air 73 seconds after liftoff, killing five NASA astronauts and two payload specialists, including Christa McAuliffe, who would have been the first teacher in space.

It is highly doubtful Father Reynolds meant to go out in such ironic flare on the same day as the explosion of an aircraft like the tragedy that wore on his mind for the better part of his adult life. Perhaps it would be more fitting for the quiet end of Father Reynolds remarkable time on Earth to be remembered in the same compassionate breath as the words he penned in the conclusion of a paper dated August, 1972.

"To keep a mental balance, and my feet on solid ground, I feed the birds: wild birds (sparrows don't count; they are insolent). A bird writer writes, 'You will succeed well with birds if you are prepared to admit that, in some things at least, they are much smarter than you are.' Seems to me that fits humans, too."

The crown witness to one of Chicago's most infamous mob hits went to his grave as the lone constant in a whirlwind of theories, conjectures, questions and debates that to this day continue to surround the plane crash that killed Knute Rockne.

Say what you will about the holy man who put up his fists at the drop of a hat and once pummeled the head of a fellow priest locked in a half-nelson, the details of the extraordinary story Father Reynolds shared with James Bacon and Kitty Gorman at the age of 39 in 1934 stayed true to the same set of facts he told to Ron Karten 52 years later at the age of 91.

Father Reynolds rests among 38 graves in the back yard of the church on the grounds of Our Lady of Guadalupe Abbey. His unwavering testament that a bomb was planted on that plane meant for either him or his pal Rockne is etched in eternity.

Section 4: The Rockne Legacy

24

HIS SPIRIT

Knute Rockne the man may have died on the morning of March 31, 1931, but it is impossible to kill a legend.

Step on the campus of the University of Notre Dame, and Rockne's presence is almost palpable. You can feel it as you walk the same paths that Rockne trod nearly a century ago. You enter Notre Dame Stadium, "The House That Rockne Built" and one of the true meccas of college football, and you can almost see it hovering in the sky on those sunny September Saturdays or those blue-gray October skies. If you are fortunate enough to be invited in, you can almost touch it in the locker room where he first commanded his "Ramblers."

Captured in bronze, the spirit of Knute Rockne still manages to emit an air of greatness that stands most prominently at the north gate of Notre Dame Stadium, the Rockne Gate as it's now called. During his legendary career, Rockne amassed a winning percentage of .881 —

still unsurpassed by any coach of a major college football program nearly a century after his death. It's only fitting that a legend should be remembered for compiling the game's all-time winning percentage among college football's greatest coaches.

The statue captures Rockne -- legs shoulder width. Hands on hips. Whistle on a chain around the neck. High-top football shoes fully laced to the top. It is at once a tribute and a relic, symbolic of time past when football's cherished and most recognizable forefather woke up the country's masses to a baby game hungry for maturation. With his head slightly cocked to the side, a gentle, fatherly grin greets all who stop to pay tribute as if to say, "Nice job, kid, now do it better tomorrow."

"I was trying to make him approachable," explained artist Jerry McKenna, who was born six years after Rockne died, but has made it his life's work sculpting Rockne's invincible spirit as if he had known the legend personally.

Rockne's expression is channeled through the sculptor's artistic vision in all nine of his pieces that stand at memorials across the country and around the world. Perhaps his most relevant location serves as a bookend to the time-honored path that runs out from under the Hesburgh Library's "Touchdown Jesus" mural, across the courtyard where Rockne's teams lined up on old Cartier Field, to the Rockne Gate.

"I wanted the face to reflect a man who is approachable, and who could hold your stare for a minute," McKenna said.

There are a number of coaches in the history of college football with far more wins than Rockne's 105. However, he only had 13 seasons at Notre Dame before his untimely death.

The winningest coach is John Gagliardi, who bests all challengers with an incredible 489 wins, 138 losses and 11 ties. It took Gagliardi 64 years, coaching at Carroll College in Helena, Montana, and St. John's University in Collegeville, Minnesota, to reach that height.

Eddie Robinson deserves his own category: 408 wins, 168 losses, 15 ties. The iconic head coach of Grambling State University turned his historic Black college into a college football landmark just as Rockne turned his historic Catholic institution into college football lore.

There's Penn State's Joe Paterno and the major college football reality of 401 wins, 135 losses and 3 ties. Amos Alonzo Stagg's 329 wins; Paul "Bear" Bryant's 325 victories; Pop Warner and his 318 wins; all top Rockne's total of 105 wins.

But to this day, Rockne's .881 winning percentage remains the best of the best of the top-tier coaches in college football history. In his brief tenure at Notre Dame from 1918 to 1930, Knute Rockne held the nation captive with 105 wins, 12 losses, five ties, five undefeated seasons without a tie, and three national championships.

And there was so much more.

From selling Notre Dame as a commercial football brand all across the country to redesigning the shape of the ball itself to fit more comfortably in the quarterback's passing hand, Rockne's imprint on the game itself remains firmly stamped on the mass audience that makes up modern-day American sports culture. The spirit of Rockne remains as strong as it is timeless.

"A lot of what he started here is what we, as coaches, try to carry on with tradition and exccllence," said former Notre Dame All-American defensive back Todd Lyght, as he stood a few feet away from the Rockne statue following a youth football seminar at the stadium in June 2018.

"He is the genesis for everything Notre Dame football is today."

The indelible imprint Rockne left on Fighting Irish football barely scratches the surface of the influence his spirit still carries to an entire country. Often overlooked is the fact that in a nation reeling from the Great Depression, Rockne's teams provided a much-needed diversion.

His coaching legend spans every level of the game, and sports in general with all of its pom-poms, circumstance and glory. Rockne's indomitable spirit is still called on whenever a leader of athletes, corporate sales employees or military soldiers needs to serve up motivation. Anytime a coach or manager in any sport delivers a stirring locker room speech, the spirit of Rockne is conjured to inspire the troops just as Rockne so famously did in 1928 during halftime in the locker room at Yankee Stadium when the Irish were deadlocked in a scoreless battle with staunch rival Army.

That day, the stirring eloquence of Rockne spawned a blueprint for motivation. Believe in the actual happening or dismiss it as an illusion of hype created by Hollywood and perpetuated by cultural myth, but there isn't a coach in any sport who hasn't at one time or another conjured the Rockne spirit to:

"Win one for the Gipper …"

25

SHAPING FOOTBALL

K nute Rockne did not invent the game of football.

American football traces its origins back to mid-19th century Britain and early versions of rugby and association football — both of which utilized a rounded, fat football kicked at a goal or over a line in an assortment of varieties.

College football had already achieved a level of supreme popularity throughout the United States by the turn of the century in 1900, largely due to the coaching innovations of Walter Camp, widely regarded as the "Father of American Football." Camp, head coach at Yale University and a Hopkins School graduate, instituted the Americanized game's first rules by introducing a line of scrimmage, downs, distance parameters, and the legalization of blocking.

If there were a Mount Rushmore for college football coaches, Rockne's visage would certainly be carved in stone alongside Camp, Glenn Scobey "Pop" Warner and Amos Alonzo Stagg — with Rockne being the most recognizable. The figure of Rockne in his trademark overcoat and tie, hat over a prematurely bald head and a wide flat-nosed boxer's mug remains the face of college football, transcending his era from 1918 to his final national championship season of 1930.

Like baseball's Babe Ruth, who during the same time period drove the game Abner Doubleday created into a primetime show of competition, the product Rockne put on the field was a spectacular display that sold tickets by the thousands, introduced college football to a national audience, and elevated Notre Dame to the college football stratosphere along with every school that played the Fighting Irish on any given Saturday afternoon.

Rockne may not have invented the game of football. But he was the first to breathe air into its shape — literally.

The first ball used in the game's infancy was round, but quickly reshaped into the semblance of a swollen watermelon made from a pig's bladder. In addition to bulky handling issues, one constant problem involved inflation, especially when the passing game was used more frequent during the second decade of the 1900s.

While Rockne coached Notre Dame football, his business interests included a football clothing line he designed and marketed through Wilson Sporting Goods. Rockne's clothing line carried the first football pants with pads sewn into a protective waistline.

In 1924, Wilson Sporting Goods introduced the Rockne Double-Lace football. Rockne had worked with Wilson to design the Wilson-Rockne Ball - a sleek pigskin leather model held together by thick cross-stitched lacing in the middle and a brand-new feature never before seen on a football: an air valve to regulate inflation.

"The Rockne Double-Lace method is an exclusive Wilson feature found only on Wilson-Rockne Official Footballs," Wilson announced in advertisements when the new ball was first introduced to the public. "The feature combined with the patented Wilson Double Lining and air-valve features place the Wilson-Rockne Ball in a class all by itself. It's the ultimate in a football. Perfectly shaped and keeps it shape longer than any ball made — the double lacing and double lining methods are the reasons why it is known as the 'The Perfect Foot Ball.'"

The modern football carries Rockne's handprint on the air valve. Why, if it weren't for Knute Rockne, today's fans may have never heard of "Deflategate."

26

PERFECTING THE PASS

Contrary to popular football mythology, Knute Rockne did not create the forward pass.

The concept of throwing a football spiral with an overhand motion was first drawn up in 1903 by two men — Howard R. "Bosey" Reiter of Wesleyan University, and Eddie Cochems, head coach at St. Louis University. Cochems' St. Louis University quarterback Bradbury Robinson completed the first legal forward pass in a game on Sept. 5, 1906, a 20-yarder to Jack Schneider that drew very little attention outside the stadium that day, and virtually no mention in the press.

A year later, the forward pass received its most notable public indoctrination with Pop Warner's revolutionary single-wing system — dubbed "the Carlisle Formation" — at Pennsylvania's Carlisle Indian Industrial School.

Carlisle featured the legendary Jim Thorpe, arguably the greatest athlete who ever graced a football field and the most powerful athletic force on any field, baseball diamond or running track in the world. Carlisle staggered opponents throughout the 1907 season by using the forward pass with such overwhelming success that one New York Herald sportswriter deemed Carlisle's passing dominance as "child's play... any down and in any emergency, and it was seldom that they did not make something with it."

Warner's Carlisle Formation was also successful because the forward pass was such a new concept. Most teams were rendered helpless against the pass since opposing coaches had yet to design defenses to counteract even the most primitive passing schemes — most of which consisted of short pitches, shovel passes and primitive passing routes that involved the receiver running downfield a few yards to a spot, then waiting stationary for the ball to be thrown.

Knute Rockne and his best friend, speedy Notre Dame quarterback Gus Dorais, began practicing with each other privately during the summer of 1913 when Rockne was working a summer job as a lifeguard on the beach - and both split-time working as waiters — at a summer resort at Cedar Point not far from Sandusky, Ohio

When the dishes were washed and packed away, Rockne and Dorais donned bathing suits and went swimming, always with a football in hand. Coming out of the water, the two would throw the football back and forth for an hour at a time. Day after day, workout after workout, in the water and on land, Dorais and Rockne relentlessly ran their own conceived passing drills. With Dorais passing, Rockne devised his own set of patterns. Sometimes he would run to a spot and turn around. Other times, Rockne ran a route without stopping as Dorais timed his pass in the air so that Rockne could run under it without breaking stride.

Those workout sessions not only elevated the forward pass to a new level, they gave birth to what is known in modern football as the "route tree."

Dorais-to-Rockne was the most sophisticated forward passing combination in all of football going into 1913. Later that year, Rockne and Dorais unleashed their newfound passing schemes on Army, shocking the college football powerhouse 35-13 in a game that drew national sports headlines. Dorais completed 14 of 17 passes for 243 yards, mostly to Rockne, and stamped the forward passing system with the timed running route as football's most lethal offensive weapon.

The genesis of the forward pass transported into the revelation set by Dorais and Rockne. Other teams were quick to follow, and the results would soon transpire with success in various parts of the country. But that was merely the beginning of the Rockne influence on intercollegiate football.

Advances in the forward-passing movement arrived swiftly. The rules were changed to eliminate penalties for incompletions and throwing the ball over the center of the line, which opened the gates for the forward pass to become football's most exciting reason to buy a ticket.

The Dorais-to-Rockne game also served as a cornerstone in displaying the potency of the forward pass with an "open offense," prompting many coaches across the country to add passing plays designed with the running route to their playbooks.

27

GOLD AND BLUEPRINTS

As a coach, Rockne's innovative schemes laid strategic blueprints for the game that have been handed down and reshaped by coaches throughout the years. For instance, Rockne's 7-2-2 defensive structure was the early design for the way defensive coaches "stack the box" against a run-heavy team.

Rockne's "Notre Dame Box" offense — with the backfield lined up in a T-formation then quickly shifting into a single-wing box to the left or right of center just as the ball was snapped — arguably served as the game's first shift. Dubbed simply the "Notre Dame shift," Rockne's pre-snap shifting scheme proved so successful, it was banned by college rule-makers. Today, rules allow only one player at a time to be in motion before the snap; any additional pre-snap movement after the line is completely set draws a 5-yard penalty for a "false start."

Rockne was also the first coach to teach the "brush block," where an offensive blocker makes light contact with one opponent then continues downfield for secondary blocking. Another first — Rockne's strategy to break a team into smaller groups — became a precursor to platoon football.

His Notre Dame team was also the first to employ "shock troops," substitutes to give the starters a breather and soften up the opposition for a refreshed first team. Rockne strategically utilized second-string subs in the first and second quarters to wear down opposing teams' starters during the early part of game, then hit with first-teamers full force in the second half when the opposition's unrested starters were worn down. Today, the strategy of using "shock troops" is not only prevalent in football, but also in basketball to get starters in foul trouble early, and to a smaller degree, relief pitchers in baseball.

Rockne was also the first coach to popularize coast-to-coast schedules. Once, Rockne chided a player for "having the nerve to travel 20,000 miles with Notre Dame and still flunk geography." He was also the first coach to carry the team's own local water supply on trips.

No football coach before Rockne thought enough to make spring practice drills the toughest, most grueling sessions of the year. Rockne was the first to organize practice sessions by breaking players down into small groups according to position rather than hold mass drills. He was also the first to activate otherwise inept substitutes for away games to use them as morale builders -- Rudy, anyone?

Rockne originally enrolled in college to be a doctor, and accumulated top-of-his-class grades in biology and chemistry — a subject he would specialize in and teach as a Notre Dame professor of chemistry from 1916 until 1922 when Rockne stepped away from the classroom to serve as full-time head football coach.

He knew his oxides as well as his pigskins, and possessed a brilliant knowledge of anatomy, a mindset that allowed the coach to double as a trainer since the school couldn't afford one. In turn, Rockne was the first coach or sports trainer to perform "heroic treatment" for sprained ankles by applying wet heat then making his player walk to reinforce blood flow to the injured ankle. In addition to head football coach and chemistry instructor, Rockne served as a self-proclaimed "one-man merger" as Notre Dame's graduate manager, athletic direction, track coach, treasurer of athletic funds, trainer, waiter, valet, a literal jack of all trades unheard of in today's specialized world of major intercollegiate sports.

"When Rockne first took charge of Notre Dame football, the team had no such financial resources as it has now," former sports and magazine editor John D. McCallum wrote in "We Remember Rockne," the book he co-penned in 1975 with former Rockne player Paul Castner. "He had to be coach, trainer, rubber, ticket-taker, baggage master and financial secretary. He did everything, and this included blowing up the footballs with which the boys played."

Rockne's broad intellect was unparalleled among football coaches during his time and thereafter. Unlike most who put the game above everything, education always took priority over football. Rockne's first question to any young man who applied to him to play football at Notre Dame was: "Do you want a college education?" He had no use for players who weren't good students and couldn't keep up with their classes. Holding to the idea that "a good student is a good athlete," Rockne always put brains at a premium.

But the nail Rockne forever hung his famous hat on was the same nail he first hammered during those summer workout sessions at Cedar Point with Dorais. Rockne coached the passing scheme he and Dorais had devised as players. Expanding a repertoire of patterns to fit into his pioneering offensive system was like nurturing, cultivating, and perfecting his child.

Today, there isn't a modern football team anywhere — pee wee, Pop Warner League, high school, college or professional — that doesn't prioritize the forward pass as an integral part of the offensive system. In the NFL, the best passing systems now utilize the timing route — a synchronized system of routes being run at the same time with the quarterback reading the defensive coverage and throwing the ball to what is anticipated will be an open spot on the field.

If the passing route schemes Rockne devised — first with Dorais as a college player, and later as mastermind of Notre Dame's shift offense — have one profound impact on the game, it's this: The running game grinds out yards on the ground and buys time off the clock — the forward pass sells tickets.

28

THE GREAT MOTIVATOR

Knute Rockne was the antithesis of his own classic image.

A shy, self-effacing anomaly who sounded through a staccato-pitched stammer that heightened to a screech instead of a clamor, Rockne didn't even look the part of the greatest football coach in the land nor the game's most prodigious endorser.

He stood only 5-feet, 8 inches tall although some who knew him said he was shorter, perhaps the result of a pair of spindly legs that had been bowed and nearly crippled from severe phlebitis. A nose that had been crushed when he was a teen by either a baseball bat in a brawl or a foul tip off a bat while positioned as a catcher during a pickup sandlot game left Rockne with the flattened mug of a back-alley fighter. When he entered Notre Dame at the age of 21, Rockne had already started to go bald which made him look at least 10 years older all the way up to his death at 43.

"The first time I saw Rockne, he looked like a man far too old for college," Gus Dorais once said. "He was wearing blue cord pants, held up with white leather suspenders. He had on a light blue jersey with a black cap. He could have passed for a race track tout."

Rockne's sharp wit, keen intellect and engaging charm belied his appearance as a poor man's commoner. He took great pains trying to improve his physical appearance, spending hundreds of dollars on hair restoratives and consulting a plastic surgeon in Chicago about his nose. The coach outlined his struggles to refine his public speaking skills in an unfinished autobiography that was published in Collier's magazine under the title, "Knute Rockne, His Life and Legend."

But anyone who dared to call out Rockne's physical traits in public drew the coach's infamous wrath.

"He looks like an old, punched-up preliminary fighter who becomes door-tender in a speakeasy," wrote Westbrook Pegler, the one-time Chicago Tribune scribe who usually saved his poison pen for presidents from both parties, the tax system and corrupt labor unions. "He sits at a shadowy table in a corner near the door at night, recalling the time he fought Billy Papke in Peoria for $50. No one would ever suspect that Knute Rockne was a great football coach. He simply refuses to act or look the part."

A furious Rockne never spoke to Pegler again. Nevertheless, in the wake of Rockne's death, Pegler wrote:

"I read that youth has no idols nowadays. But they had one at Notre Dame."

As a leader of young men, football never knew a more skillful field tactician, or a more powerful motivator. To this day Rockne's immortal speeches continue to stand over the test of time influencing every facet of life whenever a leader — from coaches, managers and military generals, to corporate CEOs — needs to inject a charge into the troops.

Rockne was not hesitant to stretch the truth to get his point across when the moment required an urgent spark. Former players readily recalled that Rockne said whatever he thought he had to say to ignite his team, whether he made up a story about his 6-year-old son being hospitalized or implying that Indiana's ferocious tackling style may have contributed to the death of George Gipp even though Gipp had succumbed to a strep throat infection compounded by the onset of pneumonia. Even Rockne's claim of being at Gipp's bedside to hear the dying words he would use eight years later during the famous "Win one for the Gipper" speech has provoked questions of truthfulness.

"They were all lies, blatant lies," recalled Jim Crowley, a member of Notre Dame's famed Four Horsemen backfield, speaking to a sports publication years after Rockne's death. "The Jesuits call it mental reservation, but he had it in abundance."

Perhaps 'exaggeration' warrants a more accurate description of Rockne's motivational tactics.

Little Billy Rockne had actually seen a doctor to remove a peanut stuck in his nose when Notre Dame traveled two days by train to play Georgia Tech in 1922, a powerhouse team that was heavily favored by 35 points against Rockne's Irish squad largely made up of first-year players. Rockne may have stretched the severity of his family situation a bit, but being a master motivator provided Rockne with the mental reservation to shift his fatherly concerns for his son into a general's charged attempt to light a fire under his underdog team.

"Rockne came into that dressing room before the game-time and he had a great number of telegrams in his right hand," Crowley recalled. "He said they were from all over the country. In his left hand held a lone wire. He said it was from his poor sick little boy, Billy, who was critically ill back in the hospital in South Bend. And then he read the wire. The lips began to tremble. A lump came to a throat. He says, 'I want Daddy's team to win.'"

Don Miller's recollection differed slightly than his Four Horsemen teammate Crowley's, but both shared the same reverent understanding of their beloved coach's method.

"I'll never forget the way he unfolded that one," Miller recounted in an interview years later. "Sort of hesitantly, and I'd have sworn his hands trembled a bit. It seemed he couldn't make up his mind whether he really wanted to read this one, but he did… 'It's just from my son, Billy,' Rock told us. 'Billy is ill and has been taken to the hospital.' He then read the telegram. It said, 'Please win this game for my daddy. It's very important to him.'"

Rockne's absolute truth that day paled in comparison to his plea for accomplishment. His son's presumed plight cut right to the jugular of his players' competitive souls.

"We all knew Billy, of course," Miller said. "He was Rock's little 4-year-old, a tow-headed kid who often came to watch us at practice, a great favorite of the players. Well, I'll tell you, it really got us.

"Rock didn't say another word, just put the telegram back in his pocket and walked out. We burst out after him onto the field, yelling and cursing our heads off.

"We tore that Georgia Tech team apart and beat 'em 13-3," Miller added. "They never had a chance."

And when the train carrying the victorious Irish football squad pulled into Union Station in South Bend the following Monday, the first one to beat the crowd and run up to his father "whooping and hollering" was Billy Rockne.

"You never saw a healthier kid in all your life," Crowley recalled. "He hadn't been in a hospital since the week he was born. But the guys on the team never considered they'd been taken in by Rock. There wasn't even anything to forgive… and we'd find out over the couple of years that Rock would use any ploy he could think of to get the most out of us, whether it was at practice or in a game."

Rockne's truth was never challenged more than his narrative of the fabled George Gipp, although Hollywood, not Rockne, catapulted "… win one for the Gipper…" into eternity as the undisputed king of motivational speeches. Pat O'Brien as Rockne standing somberly at bedside leaning his ear into the dying words of Ronald Reagan as Gipp in the film "Knute Rockne: All-American" was the epitome of heart-wrenching drama when it was released to a national film audience in 1940, nearly a decade after Rockne's death.

The truth?

Had Rockne been anything less than the celebrated salesman he portrayed during his epic life, anything less than the savvy persuader who sold everything from Studebaker automobiles, to a line of sporting goods, to his own football teams on storming out of a locker room and destroying their opponents, Hollywood would never had wasted one cent to make a feature film on the life of Knute Rockne.

Where's that Hollywood bio-feature on Pop Warner or Tad Jones? And if Rockne hadn't been the charismatic superstar of his time who turned a few spirited words into Notre Dame legend every weekend for 13 consecutive autumns, the Gipper himself may have lost out on the immortality that launched his name into the eternal blueprint of every coach's most passionate call to arms.

Rockne's secret lay in his relentless pursuit of keeping his players tightly focused on their upcoming rival.

"The report that one time after he'd lost a ballgame, they rode the train someplace," recalled Don Hamilton, quarterback of the undefeated Notre Dame team in 1909 who served as an assistant coach in 1912 when Rockne was a player, during an interview shortly before his death in 1959. "He'd put up a photograph of each man's opponents in the sleeper so that that fellow could look at him last thing before he went to sleep, and first thing when he woke up in the morning."

Rockne's motivational magic was caste in his impeccable timing.

Gipp died in December 1920. Rockne, being a firm believer in holding his right words for the right time, let eight years go by before he pulled Gipp — his ace of spades — out of his motivation deck. Notre Dame was up against powerhouse Army on November 10, 1928, in Yankee Stadium. They had entered the game as heavy underdogs, but had battled Army to a scoreless tie in the first half. Rockne's men needed every volt of charge he could ignite before they took the field for what promised to be a brutal second half.

At halftime, the players huddled around Rockne in the locker room, sitting on old dusty blankets from World War I that covered a cold floor. Rockne lowered his head. There was a pause before he began speaking slowly in his familiar nasal staccato. None of the players had known Gipp personally, but every one of them knew his greatness. They listened in solemn silence as their great coach recounted what Gipp had said to him on his dying bed.

"I've got to go, Rock. It's all right, I'm not afraid. Sometime, Rock, when the team is up against it, when things are wrong and the breaks are beating the boys, tell them to go in there with all they've got and win just one for the Gipper. I don't know where I'll be then, Rock, but I'll know about it, and I'll be happy.

"The day before he died, George Gipp asked me to wait until the situation seemed hopeless," Rockne continued. His voice rose to a resounding alarm. "This is the day… and you are the team!"

Whether Rockne exaggerated the truth for his own motivational gain to light a charge into his Fighting Irish that day didn't matter. His players were transcended into a do-or-die call to battle in the name of Gipp.

"There was no one in the room that wasn't crying," assistant coach Ed Healey recalled years later. "There was a moment of silence, and then all of a sudden those players ran out of the dressing room and almost tore the hinges off the door. They were all ready to kill someone."

Army jumped out to a 6-0 lead in the second half, but fate never gave them a chance. Notre Dame scored two touchdowns and stymied a last-minute rally to beat the Cadets 12-6. When Jack Chevigny plunged over the goal line for a touchdown to tie the score at 6-6, the star running back jumped up in the end zone and shouted, "That's one for the Gipper!"

But as fate would have it, it was a reserve named Johnny "One-Play" O'Brien - a skinny hurdler on the track team who earned his nickname because he was normally used for only one play during a football game - who came off the bench and sealed the deal for the Irish. After O'Brien cradled a wobbly pass from halfback Butch Niemiec on the 10-yard line and crossed the goal line for the winning touchdown, Chevigny screamed from the sidelines, "That's one for the Gipper too!"

"You could see a great big smile on his face," quarterback Frank Carideo recalled to an interviewer years later. "He was happy when things created during the week were used to perfection in the ballgame."

For Rockne, the only truth was winning.

29

DISCIPLES

COACH OF COACHES

Two years after graduating from Notre Dame and a storied college football career as a member of the Four Horsemen, Harry Stuhldreher weighed his options between playing professional football and coaching in 1926.

His mentor offered some sage advice.

"If you plan to make a career of coaching, don't play," Knute Rockne told his former star quarterback. "If you are going into business, play and make the money as long as you can, and it's honest."

Coaching football was Rockne's business. Within three years, his national prominence had grown profoundly as the premiere coach in the country and his public acclaim had already reached new heights as a motivational speaker, so Rockne launched his first coaching school at Culver Military Academy in Culver, Indiana.

The Rockne Coaching Schools quickly blossomed into a mandatory offseason learning session for hundreds of students across the country. Attendees paid $25 for the clinic, $25 for room and board, and they received two college credits in physical education to sit in on two weeks of classroom lectures and participate in hands-on drills taught by the greatest football coach in America.

Spanning nine years from 1922 until his death in 1931, Rockne took his summer clinics to 17 different schools throughout the United States: From William and Mary, Bucknell, and Washington & Lee in the East; to Southern Methodist in the South; from Wittenberg in Ohio, to Hastings in Nebraska; and West to Southern California and Oregon State. Rockne even landed across the Pacific in Hawaii for a series of clinics.

Occasionally, Rockne teamed with fellow coaching pal Pop Warner to conduct the Warner-Rockne Coaching School, which also encompassed basketball. Notre Dame basketball coach George Keogan headed the basketball segment of the schools before Rockne partnered with his friend W. E. "Doc" Meanwell, head basketball coach at the University of Wisconsin, to form the Rockne-Meanwell Schools in 1927.

The operation was one of Rockne's most lucrative financial endeavors. By 1927, the Rockne-Meanwell Schools cleared nearly $27,000 a year in profits, while Rockne's home clinic at Notre Dame brought in an additional $10,000 to $15,000 in annual revenues. Rockne's fee to speak at other coaching schools around the country was a flat $2,000.

But Rockne saved his personal best for those who played under his leadership at Notre Dame - four years of football tutelage that benefited his players greatly upon graduation. Colleges throughout the country openly sought players out of Notre Dame simply because they had played for Rockne. Irish players, in return, worked harder in practice and concentrated on learning everything they could from their master mentor with the full realization that they would be in high demand for a coaching job the minute they got their degree from Notre Dame.

Out of respect for the unparalleled football brilliance he handed down to all of his players at Notre Dame, Rockne was the first call for coaches and athletic directors from other schools seeking a graduating player who might be a potential coaching candidate.

After they were off and growing into their own coaching wings, Rockne made sure to stay in his pupils' lives and help them move up the coaching ladder. He spoke at their team banquets, lent advice on coaching and even personal family matters, and helped them acquire new coaching positions.

Rockne's recommendation launched Jim Crowley from assistant coach at the University of Georgia to the head coaching job at Michigan State. Rockne also had a hand in helping Elmer Layden land his first head coaching position at Duquesne, telling his former star Four Horseman, "They will give you full leeway — make sure you hire a couple of Notre Dame men to help you."

Rockne's one condition to former players he pushed into the coaching ranks, and to presidents of other universities, was simple: "Hire a couple of Notre Dame men." In return, Rockne's guys were the first to offer their mentor scouting reports of other teams.

It's why Rockne's coaching tree stands tallest and casts the widest shadow of legacy over the archives of college football to this day. In just 13 seasons as head coach of America's most relevant football team of the time, Rockne launched 50 proteges into head coaching careers, and more than 150 into college and high school programs as assistant coaches.

Nine — Hunk Anderson, Charlie Bachman, Harry Baujan, Gus Dorais, Frank Leahy, Slip Madigan, Jim Phelan, Buck Shaw and Frank Thomas — are enshrined as coaches in the College Football Hall of Fame. Four men under Rockne — Anderson, Shaw, Adam Walsh and Curly Lambeau — went on to coach in the NFL.

Adding more shadow under the legacy tree cultivated by the ultimate coaches' coach, the Notre Dame system was adopted by thousands of high school, college and professional instructors who attended the Rockne Coaching Schools.

Harry Stuhldreher took Rockne's advice to Villanova University, where he landed almost immediately after graduating from Notre Dame to serve as head coach from 1925 to 1935. The Four Horsemen's quarterback then coached the University of Wisconsin-Madison from 1936 to 1948. He retired after compiling a career coaching record of 110-87-15.

GUS DORAIS

Dorais to Rockne…

In a parallel universe the two would be spoken in the same breath together, forever… Dorais and Rockne, like pass and catch.

Army didn't know what hit them on November 1, 1913. All game long Knute Rockne sprinted past Army's secondary defenders at full speed, and all game long Gus Dorais threw pass, after pass, after pass, and hit either Rockne, Joe Pliska or Charles Finegan in full stride, seemingly play after play after play.

Notre Dame unleashed the force of football future on Army that day. Dorais' passing statistics - 14 completions out of 17 throws for 243 yards and three touchdowns — may as well had been numbers he tossed out of an infinitesimal calculus theorem. Nobody before had ever seen such alien passing stats come out of a single game. By the time undefeated powerhouse Army realized they were on the helpless end of a 35-13 thrashing, Dorais to Rockne had given birth to the forward pass as a dynamic football system.

While Rockne possessed the cerebral vision to devise plays and schemes as a player and taught Dorais how to grip the football to be thrown farther and more accurately during those famous 1913 summer workouts at Cedar Point, Gus Dorais rolled into Notre Dame from Chippewa Falls,

Wisconsin, with a stunning set of physical skills facilitated by a slight 5-feet-7, 135-pound frame.

Rockne's renown would come later as a storied coach; Dorais was Notre Dame's undisputed star for three consecutive undefeated seasons that began his sophomore year in 1911 and ended after his senior season in 1913 with a record of 20-0-2 as a starting quarterback.

Versatility with a keen fundamental understanding of every position set Dorais apart from the college game's biggest stars at the time. In addition to quarterback, Dorais served as the team's punter, place kicker and punt returner, and he was a stellar defensive back. Lost in the spotlight of the unprecedented passing numbers Dorais put up against Army was an interception he picked off in the Notre Dame endzone deep in the game that ended an Army drive.

When Dorais was selected as a first-team All-American in 1913 by Walter Camp and the International News Service, he became the first consensus All-American in Notre Dame history. Louis "Red" Salmon was named to Walter Camp's third-team All-American squad in 1903 to become Notre Dame's first official All-American player. When Dorais was selected to the 1913 All-American team by Walter Camp and the International News Service, he became Notre Dame's first "consensus" All-American named by two or more NCAA-sanctioned selection committees.

Dorais to Rockne took the forward pass into professional football in 1915. Despite his feathery weight of 138 pounds, Dorais quickly entrenched himself as one of the pro game's most exciting stars, playing for the Massillon

Tigers in 1915, 1918 and 1919, and the Fort Wayne Friars in 1916. During the 1915 season, Dorais and Rockne teamed up for perhaps pro football's first genuine passing combo in a season highlighted by two games against the Canton Bulldogs, which featured the player Rockne viewed as the greatest to ever put on a uniform — Jim Thorpe.

Dorais and Rockne played together into the pros, and they set out on the same coaching career path together. Dubuque College, a Catholic college in Dubuque, Iowa, was Dorais first coaching stop. As versatile in coaching as he was as a player, Dorais served as the school's coach for football, basketball and track, as well as athletic director, teacher, and chairman of commercial law.

Before leaving Dubuque for the U.S. Army in December 1917, Dorais compiled a 17-9-2 record as head football coach, including one undefeated season in 1916. His basketball teams won Hawkeye Conference championships in each of his three seasons at the helm.

Rockne and Dorais came together again in September 1919 when Rockne, who had been named Notre Dame head coach in 1918, hired Dorais as his assistant. Their coaching combination proved as lethal as their passing combination as they led the 1919 Notre Dame team to a perfect 9-0 record. Dorais also took over as head coach of Notre Dame's basketball and baseball teams.

In May 1920, the parallel football universe Dorais and Rockne had been residing in together for the better part of a decade split one-way west when Dorais was hired as athletic director at Gonzaga University in Spokane. While

Rockne stayed put at Notre Dame until his death 11 years later, Dorais coached Gonzaga's football, basketball, baseball and track teams so successfully for five years, boosters helped raise his salary from $4,000 to $7,000 to keep him for a fifth season in 1924. Dorais guided the football team to an undefeated season in 1924 led on the field by Houston Stockton, the grandfather of future NBA Hall of Famer John Stockton.

When Dorais headed back to the Midwest in February 1925, the University of Detroit was launched onto the same level with Rockne's Notre Dame as one of the country's top tier of college football programs. Dorais served as the University of Detroit's athletic director and head football coach for 18 seasons until 1942, compiling a record of 113-48-7 playing against powerhouses such as Notre Dame, Army, Michigan State and Arkansas, plus regular series against major Catholic colleges and universities that included Fordham, Boston College and Catholic University.

Like Rockne's teams, losses by Dorais' squads were scarce. Between October 1927 and November 1929, Dorais' University of Detroit teams went unbeaten during a winning stretch that lasted 22 games and included a perfect 9-0 season in 1928.

And like Rockne, Dorais had an innate knack for recruiting and coaching elite athletes, particularly players who could throw the ball. Among the finest football players who played under Dorais at the University of Detroit were Lloyd Brazil, an All-American halfback in 1928 and 1929 and a NCAA passing leader in 1928; and halfback Doug

Nott, who was among the NCAA's passing leaders in 1933. As head coach of the college team for the fourth College All-Star Game at Soldier Field in Chicago in 1937, Dorais watched his quarterback Sammy Baugh lead the college stars to a 6-0 win over Curly Lambeau's Green Bay Packers — the first college All-Star team to beat the pros.

The pros called again in January 1943. Dorais left the University of Detroit to become head coach, general manager and part owner of the National Football League's Detroit Lions. The year before, the Lions recorded an abysmal 0-11 season. Dorais took over and the Lions immediately improved to 3-6-1. The following two years, Dorais put the Lions on the right path, leading them to second-place finishes two years in a row with records of 6-3-1 and 7-3. Small wonder that Dorais was credited by sportswriters with formulating "the best pass patterns in the NFL.

Things went south quickly. The Lions dipped drastically in 1946, finishing with a 1-10 mark, nor did the team fare much better the following year with a 3-9 finish. Dorais had a fresh five-year contract he had signed prior to the 1947 season, but Lions owner Fred Mandel Jr. fired the Notre Dame legend, nonetheless.

Tragedy struck in July 1947 when Dorais' youngest son, David, drowned while swimming in Tecon Lake at the family's summer home in Otsego County, Michigan. Two years later, Dorais relocated to Wabash, Indiana, and purchased an automobile dealership with his son, William. His return to coaching as backfield coach for the Pittsburgh

Steelers ended after only a few months when Dorais announced his retirement from football.

After becoming ill with a circulatory disorder, Dorais moved to the Detroit suburb of Southfield in 1953. Charles Emile "Gus" Dorais died January 3, 1954, at the age of 62, but his revolutionary overhand spiral throwing technique and his legacy as the "father of the forward pass" continues to be passed on to new football generations with the same immortal spirit as Rockne's motivational locker room speeches.

As long as there's a quarterback throwing a football to a receiver, there will be Dorais to Rockne.

STAN COFALL

• Played for Notre Dame (1914—1916), head coach for Wake Forest (1928)

Knute Rockne was an assistant football coach, one season removed from his final game as a Fighting Irish player when Stan Cofall arrived at Notre Dame in 1914.

Cofall burst onto Cartier Field with a blast. The halfback from Cleveland scored nine touchdowns and led the Fighting Irish with 82 points his first year. The following season in 1915, Cofall matched his Notre Dame inaugural by again scoring nine touchdowns, and again leading the team in points with 71. Cofall capped a brilliant Notre Dame career his senior season in 1916 when he scored 12 touchdowns and 84 points. Notre Dame's team captain was named to several All-American squads.

After graduating from Notre Dame in 1917, Cofall went back to Ohio and quickly landed with the professional Massillon Tigers football team, doubling as a player-coach alongside teammates Knute Rockne and Gus Dorais. He took a break from football in 1918 and 1919 to serve in World War I, then returned to his hometown of Cleveland and helped organize the Cleveland Indians football team.

When Cofall traveled to Canton, Ohio in 1920 to attend the first formal meetings of the American Football Association, (the future National Football League,) he was named the league's first vice president. The same year, Cofall played for the independent Union Club of Phoenixville, an independent team that featured several players from the Buffalo All-Americans.

Cofall later played for the Union Quakers of Philadelphia, and in 1922 he joined the Pottsville Maroons and became the team's star running back, helping the Maroons become the top team in the Pennsylvania coal region. In 1924, Cofall led the Maroons to the Anthracite League championship, a precursor for the Maroons to join the NFL the following year.

Cofall followed his playing career with coaching stints at various professional and college teams. He served as head football coach at Loyola College in Maryland from 1925 to 1927, and in 1928 he took over as head football coach at Wake Forest College, now Wake Forest University.

Cofall forever remains an indelible founding father of Cleveland sports. After settling in his hometown in 1935 and founding the Stanco Oil Company, a company that would later merge with the National Solvent Corporation, Cofall worked relentlessly to bring the Notre Dame-Navy football game to Cleveland in 1942, the same year he founded the Cleveland Touchdown Club. Cofall also served as chairman of the Cleveland Boxing Commission, and he became director of liquor control for the State of Ohio.

Stanley Bingham Cofall died at his home in Peninsula, Ohio, on September 21, 1961, at the age of 68.

CHARLIE BACHMAN

• Played for Notre Dame (1914—1916), head coach for Kansas State (1920—1927), Florida (1928—1932), Michigan State (1933—1946)

Charlie Bachman was one of the coaching confidants Rockne called on in late spring of 1930 to help decide whether the Notre Dame coach was healthy enough to coach for one more season.

Like Rockne, Charles Bachman had arrived at Notre Dame from Chicago, where he had been a standout football and track athlete at Chicago's Englewood High School. At Notre Dame, Bachman played alongside Rockne in 1914, then was named an All-American at guard in 1916 during Rockne's first year as an Irish assistant coach.

After briefly setting the world record in the discus throw in 1917, Bachman spent the fall season as an assistant football coach at DePauw University. The following year, Bachman returned to the gridiron to play center for the U.S. Navy team at Great Lakes Naval Station, a team, that posted a 7-0-2 record, beating Navy, Illinois, Purdue, Mare Island

Marine Base in the Rose Bowl, and tying his former team, Notre Dame. Bachman's teammates at Great Lakes included future Chicago Bears legends Paddy Driscoll and George Halas.

At the age of 26 in 1919, Bachman took his first head coaching job at Northwestern University. He recruited a number of former players returning from World War I, but his team still was only able to win two games and lose seven.

The following season Bachman moved to Kansas State College to serve as head football coach. Over the next seven years, from 1920 to 1927, he proved that the losing record at Northwester was an aberration by posting a record of 33-23-9 at Kansas State.

Bachman moved south in 1928 when he took the head coaching job at the University of Florida in Gainesville. The Gators posted an 8-1 record in his first season, the best in Florida history at the time, and Bachman coached the school's first first-team All-American, end Dale Van Sickel, in 1929. Bachman stayed at Florida for five seasons, and posted an overall record of 27-18-3.

In spring of 1930, Bachman was on the receiving end of a letter from Rockne calling a meeting of the fabled coach's closest confidants to discuss whether he should continue coaching at Notre Dame for at least one more season while facing severe health issues. After consulting with Bachman and his other friends during that meeting, held on May 31, 1930, Rockne decided to continue coaching into the 1930 season, which would be his last.

Bachman left Florida in 1933 to become head football coach at Michigan State College in East Lansing. Under Bachman, Michigan State — which had lost to state rival Michigan for 18 years straight - defeated Michigan four consecutive seasons, from 1934 to 1937. While Bachman's Michigan State teams posted an overall record of 70-34-10, his Spartan teams were remembered for wearing gold and black uniforms instead of the school's official colors of green and white.

In 1953, Bachman took his final head coaching job at Hillsdale College in Hillsdale, Michigan. In one season, Bachman's team posted a record of 5-3-2.

Inducted into the University of Florida Athletic Hall of Fame in 1971 as an "honorary letter winner," and later into the College Football Hall of Fame in 1978, Charles Bachman died in Port Charlotte, Florida, in 1985, at the age of 93.

DUTCH BERGMAN

• Played for Notre Dame (1915—1916; 1919), head coach for Catholic (1930—1940), Washington Redskins (1943)

Dutch Bergman played halfback at Notre Dame in 1915 and 1916, and under Rockne during his second year as head coach of Notre Dame in 1919.

Born in Peru, Indiana, Bergman left Notre Dame to become head coach at the New Mexico College of Agriculture and Mechanic Arts, now New Mexico State University, from 1920 to 1922.

In 1930, Bergman took over the head coaching helm at The Catholic University of America, a coaching stint that lasted 10 years. When Bergman left the school after his final season in 1940, his Catholic Cardinals had compiled a stellar record of 59-31-4, leaving him as the winningest varsity coach in Catholic University history.

Bergman took his career college coaching record of 74-36-5 into the NFL for one season, coaching the Washington Redskins to a 6-3-1 mark in 1943 and leading them to the 1943 NFL Championship Game — a game they lost to the Chicago Bears, 41-21.

Arthur J. "Dutch" Bergman died August 18, 1972, at the age of 77. He was inducted into the Catholic University Hall of Fame in 1982.

SLIP MADIGAN

• Played for Notre Dame (1916—1917; 1919), head coach for Saint Mary's (1921—1939) Iowa (1943—1944)

The only other coach who could have taken a team that had lost one game 127-0 and turn it into a national powerhouse was Knute Rockne himself.

Slip Madigan played center for Notre Dame in 1916 and 1917, when Rockne was an assistant, then again in 1919 during Rockne's second season as Fighting Irish' head coach. Upon graduating from Notre Dame, the native of Ottawa, Illinois took the football knowledge he learned at the hands of Rockne and headed west to the San Francisco Bay area.

It didn't take long for Madigan to land a head coaching job. Little St. Mary's, a small college on the fringes of Oakland better known as St. Mary's College, was badly in need of a Notre Dame football alum with Rockne pedigree to take over a floundering football team that was coming off an epic 127-0 thrashing by California in the final game of the 1920 season.

The new coach gutted the Galloping Gaels when he took over in 1921. Madigan replaced the old squad with 60 hand-picked recruits he brought into St. Mary's to play football. He taught his new team plays he picked up from Rockne's schemes as well as some fresh ones Madigan drew up from his own vision. Among Madigan's chalkboard innovations included the "forward fumble."

Like his mentor, Madigan proved to be a silver-tongued master motivator who cultivated the press as an ally. He used that friendship throughout the '20s and '30s to push tiny St. Mary's College - with an enrollment of 500 - into the national football spotlight traveling across the country, and even the Pacific Ocean, taking on all challengers with a squad that was every bit as skilled, tough and smart as Rockne's powerful Fighting Irish.

Under Madigan, the Galloping Gaels upset Pop Warner and Stanford, 16-0, in 1927 after Stanford had appeared in the Rose Bowl. In 1931, Madigan's Gaels knocked off another Rose Bowl team, USC, 13-7. When St. Mary's finally got a chance to play in a bowl game in 1938, they gashed Texas Tech, 201-13, in the Cotton Bowl. During Madigan's time at St. Mary's from 1921 through 1939, the Gaels were one of the country's top teams compiling a record of 117 wins, 45 losses, and 12 ties.

But it wasn't just the fact that Madigan — who also coached St. Mary's basketball and baseball teams - had taken a small West Coast school and turned its fledgling football squad into a national powerhouse playing in front of record crowds even though the school didn't have its own football stadium. It was the way he did it.

Madigan was flashy, flamboyant, and quick to offer a glib quote to any newspaper reporter or radio broadcaster who needed one, and the Gaels reflected his personality on and off the field. In one of Madigan's most celebrated public moments, the fun-loving coach took his team plus 150 fans on a cross-country train trip — tagged as "the world's longest bar" - to New York for a game against Fordham. When he arrived in New York, Madigan drummed up publicity for the game by throwing a party the night before and inviting everybody from sportswriters to Babe Ruth and New York Mayor Jimmy Walker.

St. Mary's was among the poorest schools in the country, yet Madigan was one of college football's highest paid coaches. Following that game against Fordham in 1936, nearly all the profits from the game (a total of $36,420) was handed to Madigan for back salary rather than to the school's creditors.

Madigan's flamboyant presence wore thin with St. Mary's administrators. Football had taken priority over academics during the 1930s, and Madigan's football recruits were mostly non-Catholic, thuggish, and largely viewed by the school's hierarchy as unfit for college. In 1939, star halfback Mike Klotovich was kicked out of the school for disciplinary reasons. By the end of the semester, 14 other football players were suspended from athletic competition because of poor grades.

When Madigan was summarily fired in March 1940, Brother Albert Rahill, president of St. Mary's College, insisted that Madigan was "an honorable man" who had not engaged in any financial dishonesty throughout his 19-year career at the school. But the St. Mary's president added that Madigan spent money too freely, and that toward the end of his tenure at St. Mary's, he seemed more concerned with his own business enterprises than he did with his coaching obligations.

Students, however, did not take the firing of the popular Slip Madigan lightly. St. Mary's student body president told a reporter from the San Francisco Chronicle: "St. Mary's without Madigan would be like St. Mary's without the chapel."

Madigan returned to coaching in 1943 when he went to Iowa and took over as interim coach for fellow Notre Dame football alum Eddie Anderson, who was serving in World War II. The war had depleted the rosters of most college football teams across the country, and Madigan was strapped with players of mediocre talent who were playing with physical conditions that exempted them from military service.

Despite an admirable coaching job that brought out some quality performances from the 1943 Hawkeyes, the team finished just 1-6-1. Still, Madigan was brought back for the 1944 season. The Hawkeyes finished 1-7 — the lone win being an inspired 27-6 victory over Nebraska — and Madigan retired for good after he spurned Iowa's offer to coach again in 1945.

Edward Patrick "Slip" Madigan moved back to California and spent the rest of his life managing various entrepreneurial interests. He died at his home in 1966, and is buried on the grounds of the school where he made his greatest mark, St. Mary's Cemetery in Oakland.

In 1974, Madigan was inducted into the College Football Hall of Fame as a coach.

HEARTLEY "HUNK" ANDERSON

• Played for Notre Dame (1918—1921), head coach for Notre Dame (1931—1933), NC State (1934-1936

After Coach Rockne… there was Coach Anderson.

Born in Calumet, Michigan, on the Keweenaw Peninsula not far from the hometown of George Gipp, Hunk Anderson arrived at Notre Dame in 1918 and quickly earned a spot as a lineman on newly-named head coach Knute Rockne's first team.

At 5-feet, 11 inches tall and weighing a solid 170 pounds, Anderson played guard under Rockne from 1918 to 1921, a road-grader who blocked for Gipp right up to his legendary teammate's death in December 1920.

After graduating from Notre Dame, Anderson started in 32 of 39 games he played professionally for the Cleveland

Indians and Chicago Bears football teams. Anderson blocked for Gipp at Notre Dame... and he blocked for Red Grange with the Bears.

He was named to the National Football League 1920s All-Decade Team, and is one of only two players on the list that is not in the Pro Football Hall of Fame. Anderson was inducted into the College Football Hall of Fame as a player in 1974.

Anderson began his coaching career in 1928 as head football coach at Saint Louis University. Following the 1929 season, Anderson returned to Notre Dame to take a job as an assistant coach under Rockne. Upon Rockne's death, he served as head coach at Notre Dame for three seasons from 1931 to 1933, then moved to North Carolina State University where he coached from 1934 until stepping down in 1936 after compiling a career college football record of 34-34-4.

Anderson returned to the NFL in 1939 as an assistant coach for the Detroit Lions under Gus Henderson. Three years later, Anderson was named head coach of the Chicago Bears. In four seasons, from 1942 to 1945, Anderson guided the Bears to a 24-12 record, and won the 1943 NFL Championship.

Of Anderson's ability to pass on the knowledge behind the extraordinary skills that allowed him to block for two of football's greatest running backs of their day, Bears' iconic owner George Halas once said: "Whether at a collegiate or professional level, there never was a better line coach than Hunk Anderson."

Heartley "Hunk" Anderson died after a long respiratory illness in West Palm Beach, Florida on April 24, 1978. He was 79.

EDDIE ANDERSON

• Played for Notre Dame (1919—1921), head coach for Iowa (1939—1949)

Eddie Anderson followed Knute Rockne's footsteps on the gridiron and in the medical field.

A teammate of George Gipp's under Rockne from 1918 to 1921, the Mason City, Iowa, native was a consensus first-team All-American and captain of the 1921 Notre Dame football team. In Anderson's final three seasons at Notre Dame, the Irish compiled a 28-1 record, with the only loss coming to Anderson's home-state school, Iowa, in 1921.

After graduating from Notre Dame, Anderson played professionally for the Rochester Jeffersons in the National Football League. He returned to Iowa to coach Columbia College in Dubuque to a 16-6-1 record from 1922 to 1924. The following year Anderson served as a player/coach for the professional Chicago Cardinals during the Chicago team's controversial 1925 championship season.

The same year, Anderson decided to follow the medical path Rockne had pondered upon his own graduation from Notre Dame and enrolled at Rush Medical College in Chicago. While studying to be a doctor, Anderson also coached basketball at DePaul University from 1925 to 1929, leading them to a four-year record of 25-21 before he took a job as head football coach at the College of the Holy Cross in Massachusetts.

In six years at Holy Cross from 1933 to 1938, Anderson guided his football teams to a record of 47-7-4, including two undefeated seasons in 1935 and 1937 — all while heading up the eye, ear, nose and throat clinic at Boston's Veterans Hospital.

Anderson returned home once again in 1939 when he was named head football coach at the University of Iowa. In true Rockne form, Anderson took a dismal football team that had finished 2-13-1 in two previous years and turned it around immediately by playing only the starters for significant amounts of time.

Of 85 players who showed up for spring practice, only 37 earned football letters under Anderson during his first season in 1939. Those starters, nicknamed the "Ironmen," powered one of Iowa's greatest teams in school history to a 6-1-1 record, led by 1939 Heisman Trophy winner, Nile Kinnick, and a first-year coach who was named national coach of the year by several organizations.

"It's doubtful if any coach in football history ever accomplished such an amazing renaissance as Eddie Anderson has worked at Iowa," sportswriter Jim Gallagher wrote in the Chicago Herald-American.

Before Anderson headed to the football field to coach the Iowa Hawkeyes in the afternoon, he spent mornings practicing medicine and studying urology under the head of urology at University of Iowa Hospital. He took a leave of absence from the school to serve in the U.S. Army Medical

Corps during World War II, from 1943 to 1945. When Anderson returned in 1946, he was told that if he retired from coaching, he would be named successor to the head of urology.

As Rockne had turned down medical school at St. Louis to continue coaching football, Anderson said no to the University of Iowa Hospital's offer. He continued practicing medicine part-time, and returned to coach the Hawkeyes for a second stint that lasted three years until Holy Cross offered Anderson the opportunity to return, including another stint as head football coach.

Anderson spent 15 seasons at Holy Cross, from 1950 to 1964, and posted a record of 82-60-4. He resigned at Holy Cross in 1964 after compiling a career record of 201-128-15 in 39 seasons at four schools, the fourth coach in college football history to reach 200 wins.

Upon leaving Holy Cross, Anderson was named the chief of outpatient services at the Veterans Administration Medical Center in Rutland, Massachusetts. He also served a school for mentally-challenged children.

Eddie Anderson was inducted into the College Football Hall of Fame as a coach in 1971. He passed away of a heart attack at his home in Clearwater, Florida, in 1974, at the age of 73.

HARRY MEHRE

Harry Mehre is forever etched in newspaper print as one of the country's premiere sportswriters of his time.

"Auburn and Ole Miss are two teams that defense forgot, or else the Tigers and the Rebs just forget defense for the day, as they swapped touchdowns in the Gator Bowl's 26th annual classic," Mehre wrote in his column for the Atlanta Journal-Constitution following the 1971 Gator Bowl.

"Pat Sullivan and Archie Manning put on their show and were as good as advertised. Oh, yes, Auburn won, 35-28."

In the fall of 1918, half-a-century before Harry Mehre covered that 1971 Gator Bowl in his column for the Atlanta Journal-Constitution, the dual-sport high school basketball and football star from Huntington, Indiana entered Notre Dame on a basketball scholarship.

Like the typical teenage Indiana boy at the turn of the 20th Century, Mehre grew up playing basketball. He attracted the attention of several colleges, including Notre Dame, as a basketball star at Huntington High School. Mehre also played football at the school — until his senior year when the sport was suspended following the death of a player.

Knute Rockne could spot a potential football player in any sport. It didn't take long for the first-year head coach to notice the Irish basketball team's center - a solidly-built husky figure on the court who blended size and strength with swift mobility. Mehre took Rockne up on an invitation to come out for a football practice.

Because of his speed, Rockne at first positioned Mehre at fullback. But his size on top of shifty footwork skills he picked up on the basketball court made him an ideal fit for the offensive line in Rockne's "Notre Dame Box" offense, a variation of the single-wing system that opened up the passing game for quarterback (and Mehre's basketball teammate) Leonard "Pete" Bahan, and irrepressible running backs Dutch Bergman and George Gipp.

At center, Mehre backed starter Slip Madigan during his first season in 1919. And he caught up on his knowledge of football fundamentals by learning from the indomitable Madigan, and directly from Rockne, who handled both head- and offensive line-coaching duties.

"Big, heavy and fast…" is how the 1920 Notre Dame Football Review described Mehre's performance in 1919, a season that ended with the Irish undefeated at 9-0, yet tied for a national championship with Harvard's 9-0-1 squad in polls delivered by the National Championship Foundation and Parke H. Davis. "Harry Mehre played center like a regular whenever called upon during the season, and that was quite a few times… Mehre was a valuable asset to Rockne's section gang."

Mehre only got better in 1920. He stepped into the starting center position next to Buck Shaw and Hunk Anderson on an Irish offensive line that blocked for strong-armed quarterback John Mohardt and everybody's consensus All-American, George Gipp. Although Notre Dame finished undefeated at 9-0 for the second consecutive season and, again, was named national champions in one poll and shared the championship in another, tragedy struck when Gipp died.

By his senior season in 1921, Mehre was an All-American center who knew the intricacies of Rockne's dominant "Notre Dame Box" system inside and out. Like others who had graduated from Rockne's exclusive system, Mehre had colleges across the country lined up for his services with coaching offers. He landed his first coaching job at St. Thomas College in 1923, and doubled as a player/coach for the independent professional team, the Minneapolis Marines.

Mehre's Notre Dame pedigree drew the eye of Rockne's pal George "Kid" Woodruff, head coach at the University of Georgia. Woodruff had walked away impressed with Mehre after Notre Dame dominated Georgia rival Georgia Tech, 35-7, with the "Notre Dame Box" offensive system.

Woodruff not only hired Mehre as an assistant in 1924, he also brought in Mehre's Four-Horsemen teammate Jim Crowley. Three years later in 1927, Woodruff left Georgia to pursue private business. Mehre was named Georgia's head coach on Woodruff's recommendation.

For nearly a decade, Mehre led the Bulldogs to an overall record of 59-34-6. The most memorable game during Mehre's Georgia tenure was the first game played at the new Sanford Stadium on October 12, 1929, against the Yale Bulldogs. Georgia beat Yale, 15-0, in a game later billed as "one of the greatest football spectacles ever in the South." To this day the game is memorialized by Georgia loyalists as the most memorable day in Georgia's illustrious football history.

"Christopher Columbus discovered America on October 12, 1492," Mehre would later write in his column. "On October 12, 1929, 437 years later, Yale University came to Athens, Georgia and discovered Sanford Stadium."

Football wasn't the only sport Mehre would lead at Georgia. In 1932, he took the reins of the Bulldogs basketball squad in place of then-head coach Herman Stegeman. Mehre's leadership was instrumental in a 25-16 victory over hoops' powerhouse Kentucky — the first loss in legendary Coach Adolph Rupp's storied career at Kentucky.

Mehre left Georgia in 1938 and took the head football coaching job at the University of Mississippi. He got off to a flying start in the first game of his Ole Miss career when the Rebels beat the LSU Tigers, 20-7. Ole Miss also scored victories over LSU the following three seasons, the first time a Mississippi football team won over the Tigers four consecutive years.

Mehre left Ole Miss at the end of 1945 after seven seasons. He had played for — and learned from — the best in Rockne. He had served as head coach of two major football schools and set a legendary bar of his own for future Bulldogs' and Rebels' coaches with an overall record of 98-60-7. And he had kept in constant touch with his mentor through personal letters that shared scouting reports on common opponents up until the day Rockne died.

By 1946, it was time for Mehre to start a new career away from the gridiron. He moved back to Georgia and started a private business in Atlanta. But it wasn't long before the former Bulldogs coach, whose colorful wit and acute football wisdom had been likened to Rockne, was summoned back into the sports world.

Like Rockne had spotted a promising football player moving effortlessly on the basketball court, Atlanta Journal-Constitution sports editor Ralph McGill knew a capable writer who could analyze the sport he had coached for readers. McGill hired Mehre as a columnist-analyst, and for the next 25 years the sports commentary of Harry Mehre served as a staple of game insight for Georgia football fans.

Mehre served up his best material through his regular feature, "The Football Review." The old ball coach was also a regular along with a panel of sportswriters on the "Sunday Show" hosted by Furman Bisher, the iconic sports editor of the Atlanta Journal-Constitution.

Recalled Jim Minter, former Atlanta Journal executive sports editor: "Coach Mehre could hit the nail on the head better than anybody."

Harry J. Mehre died at the age of 77 on September 27, 1978 in Atlanta, seven years after he had been inducted into the Georgia Sports Hall of Fame. Eight years after his death, Butts-Mehre Heritage Hall was christened on the University of Georgia campus in Athens to honor Mehre and the coach who followed him at Georgia, Wally Butts.

"The story of Harry Mehre is quite remarkable," wrote author and historian Mark Maxwell, who penned Mehre's biography, "From Notre Dame To Georgia: Harry Mehre, The Legend." "The most important thing to understand about Harry Mehre is there's never been one like him, and there never will be."

TOM LIEB

• Played for Notre Dame (1919—1922), head coach for Loyola Los Angeles (1930—1938), Florida (1940—1945).

When Knute Rockne was sidelined in a wheelchair with health issues during the 1929 season, one of Rockne's former players — a two-time All-American who had also won a bronze medal in the discus throw at the 1924 Paris Olympics — was handed the reins to lead Notre Dame in Rockne's place.

Tom Lieb earned his coaching stripes by leading the Irish to a 9-0 season and a national championship, the first of Notre Dame's back-to-back undefeated national championship seasons. The following year, with Rockne back at the helm, Lieb's success as an interim head coach of the nation's top college football team turned into a head coaching job at Loyola University in Los Angeles.

Born in Faribault, Minnesota, Lieb was a standout baseball, football, hockey, and track and field athlete in high school before he entered Notre Dame in 1918. Lieb earned a spot as a starting offensive tackle on Rockne's first Irish squad in 1919, then went on to letter in four sports and draw accolades as a two-time football All-American during a Notre Dame career that was cut short in 1922 when he broke his leg in a game against Purdue.

While Lieb pursued graduate studies at Notre Dame, he coached both the hockey and track and field teams, and served as an assistant line coach under Rockne's football team.

Lieb was also a two-time NCAA national champion in the discus in 1922 and 1923, and a national AAU open champion in 1923 and 1924. It was Lieb who introduced the modern spin delivery of the discus throw still used today, a pioneering technique he took into the 1924 Summer Olympics in Paris competing for the United States in the discus throw. Lieb took home a bronze medal from the 1924 Olympics. Several weeks later, he broke the discus world record with a throw of 156 feet and 2 ½ inches.

Lieb headed to Wisconsin after graduating from Notre Dame to coach linemen for the Badgers. In 1929, he returned to Notre Dame as an assistant line coach under Rockne, who spent most of the season recovering from a severe case of thrombophlebitis in the leg. Loyola came calling after the Irish championship season, and Lieb jumped at the opportunity to head west for his first head coaching position.

For eight years, Lieb worked diligently to build the Loyola Lions into a football powerhouse by forging an annual West Coast rivalry with USC. He was the kind of coach who had fun with his job, often posing with lion cubs in publicity photos while guiding his teams to a 47-33-4 record between 1930 and 1938. Lieb also coached Loyola's hockey Lions to four consecutive Pacific Coast Intercollegiate League titles on the power of a 38-3-2 record.

Lieb left Loyola in 1939 when his wife got sick. After she died, he moved back east and succeeded Josh Cody as head football coach at the University of Florida in Gainesville. Lieb doubled as the school's athletic director, but he fell short of the football success he had at Loyola. When a five-year tenure that showed a below-average 20-26-1 record came to an end in 1945, Florida did not renew Lieb's contract.

Alabama was Lieb's final coaching stop. He signed on as an assistant line coach working with an old friend, former Notre Dame teammate Frank Thomas, Alabama's head coach. Lieb also headed-up Alabama's track and field squad until he retired in 1951.

Following his retirement from Alabama, Lieb returned to Los Angeles where he found work as a public speaker.

Thomas John Lieb suffered a cardiac arrest and died on April 30, 1962 at the age of 62. He was inducted posthumously into the Loyola Marymount Hall of Fame in 1987.

BUCK SHAW

• Played for Notre Dame (1919—1921), head coach for NC State (1924), Nevada (1925—1928), San Francisco 49ers (1946-1954), Philadelphia Eagles (1958- 1960).

The "Silver Fox" was tall, slender and dignified, the sideline cut of a corporate board chairman rather than one of the greatest football coaches in collegiate and professional history.

In later years when his hair had turned silvery-white, Buck Shaw roamed the sidelines in dark sport jackets, white shirts with ties knotted tight, and he hawked the field through horn-rimmed glasses that were tinted green. Of his genteel coaching manner that was as polite as his suits, a former player under Shaw's championship tenure with the

Philadelphia Eagles once said: "He's the first guy I ever played for who didn't curse his players."

Shaw may have carried his own refined verbal skills as a coach, but he got his tough-as-nails football disposition that opened holes for George Gipp from his mentor, Knute Rockne.

Born one of five children to cattle ranchers Tim and Margaret Shaw in Mitchellville, Iowa, Shaw moved with his family to Stuart, a town that had banned high school football in the wake of a player's death on the field, then re-established the sport during Shaw's senior year.

Shaw only had four games of high school football under his belt when he enrolled at Creighton University in Omaha, Nebraska, in 1918, and went out for the football team. Shaw's season ended after one game when he caught a severe case of the flu.

The following year, Shaw transferred to Notre Dame, but not to play football under Rockne, who was entering his second year as head coach. Shaw chose Notre Dame because of its track and field team. When Rockne laid eyes on the solid 6-foot,175-pound track athlete, a spot opened up on the football team.

Rockne molded Shaw into a tenacious offensive lineman — first, at left tackle in 1919 and 1920, then moving to right tackle in 1920 and 1921. As well as steamrolling holes for George Gipp for two seasons, and finishing his Notre Dame playing career as an All-American selection by "Football World Magazine," Shaw booted 38 out of 39 extra points, (a school record that stood until 1976,) and is regarded as one of Notre Dame's all-time best place kickers.

Just before graduating in the spring of Shaw's senior year, Rockne presented him with two letters from schools in need of coaches: Auburn University in Alabama, and the University of Nevada in Reno. A friend suggested to Shaw that since rugby was the only game being played in Nevada, and that American football was virtually a new sport ready to be introduced, Shaw could cut his own path out west.

"It sounded like an interesting challenge," Shaw recalled later in a 1970 interview," so I took the Nevada job as line coach."

After four years at Nevada, Shaw tried to get out of football by taking a job at an oil firm. But his old Notre Dame teammate Clipper Smith pulled him back by persuading Shaw to come to Santa Clara University and work under Smith as an assistant coach.

During his first season in 1929, the stock market crashed: "I had a heck of a time getting on my feet," Shaw explained. Since Santa Clara could only afford to hire coaches on a part-time, seasonal basis, Shaw worked for Standard Oil and served as line coach at Santa Clara at the same time until 1936 when Smith resigned for a job at Villanova. When Shaw was named head coach to replace Smith, he resigned from his job at the oil company.

Shaw formed the Broncos into a powerhouse with the same immediacy Rockne molded his star lineman straight off the track field. During his first two seasons as head coach in

1936 and 1937, Santa Clara ran off a combined 18-1 record with back-to-back victories over LSU in the Sugar Bowls of 1937 and 1938.

Shaw may also be the first coach in major college football to get sick and "phone it in" - when he stayed home and coached the team to victory on the road over the telephone. When Santa Clara cut its football program in 1942 due to the war, Shaw remained at the school to help the Army's campus physical education program.

Coaching college players taught Shaw early-on that he was no Rockne when it came to over-the-top halftime speeches, a realization that served him respectfully when he coached professional teams later in his career. "When I discovered that I wasn't (Rockne), I dropped the histrionics," Shaw said during an interview. "Heaven help you if you try anything insincere on today's players."

Before World War II ended, the Morabito brothers of San Francisco began moving to ready the San Francisco 49ers to enter a new professional league, the All-America Football Conference (AAFC). The 49ers hired Shaw, along with his Santa Clara assistant Al Ruffo, as the franchise's first head coach. The league finally got off the ground in 1946 after a delay. Shaw assumed the helm of the 49ers, and with left-handed quarterback Frankie Albert leading the way, Shaw's 49ers finished second to the Cleveland Browns four consecutive years (from 1946 to 1949) in the AAFC's Western Division. The following year, in 1950, the 49ers, the Browns and the Baltimore Colts merged with the NFL.

Shaw returned to the college ranks in 1956. He guided the Air Force Academy to a record of 6-2-1 in his first season, but the Falcons fell to a 3-6-1 finish in 1957. Shaw headed back to the pros in 1958 to take over a floundering Philadelphia Eagles team coming off a 4-8 season that was badly in need of Rockne himself to turn things around. When the Eagles lost their ninth game of the season to finish a miserable 2-9-1, Shaw locked the door and unleashed a verbal lashing on his players - many of whom had been out the night before carousing - that would have had his mentor running for cover.

"This has never happened to me before. It will never happen again," Shaw railed. "If you don't have any pride, I do. I'll be here again next year, but some you will not. We'll win if I have to use three teams — one coming, one going... and one playing."

Just two years later, powered by the heroics of quarterback Norm Van Brocklin, Tommy McDonald, and one of the greatest two-way players to ever grace a football field, Chuck Bednarik, the Eagles beat Vince Lombardi's Green Bay Packers for the 1960 NFL championship. The chairman of the board had his greatest triumph as a football coach — and he subsequently retired.

"I wanted to get out while I was ahead," reasoned Shaw, who walked away from coaching at the age of 61 with a championship ring and the AP & UPI NFL Coach of the Year award.

Shaw headed back to California, where he landed a job at a paper products company in Menlo Park. In 1962, Santa

Clara alum Sal Sanfilippo banded together with a group of former players, friends and fans of Shaw to form the Bronco Beach Foundation and begin a fund-raising effort to raise money to build a stadium at Santa Clara University in Shaw's honor.

On September 22, 1962, Santa Clara and UC Davis lined up against each other to play the first football game at Buck Shaw Stadium.

Lawrence Timothy "Buck" Shaw died from cancer at the age of 77 on March 19, 1977. The Rockne protégé known as the "Silver Fox" is a member of the Iowa Sports Hall of Fame, the San Francisco Bay Area Sports Hall of Fame, the San Jose Sports Hall of Fame, and the Santa Clara University Hall of Fame.

At Notre Dame, Shaw's legacy rests forever alongside Rockne as a member of the all-time "Fighting Irish" football team.

FRANK THOMAS

• Played for Notre Dame (1920—1922), head coach for Alabama (1931—1946)

The common branch between Knute Rockne and Bear Bryant grew from Frank Thomas.

Born in Muncie, Indiana, the youngest of six children to immigrant parents from Wales who had arrived in the U.S. just six years earlier, Thomas grew up in East Chicago where he made a name for himself as an outstanding high school football and baseball player.

He skipped his senior year to get an early start at Kalamazoo College in Michigan. For two years, Thomas starred in both sports at Kalamazoo, and he caught the attention of former Notre Dame player and Rockne pal, Chipper Smith.

On the heels of Smith's repeated urgings, Rockne got his new quarterback admitted into Notre Dame in 1919. And Thomas got a new roommate - George Gipp.

Thomas and Gipp were best friends immediately. Like Thomas, Gipp was also an outstanding baseball player, and both played professional baseball in the off-season. Together at Notre Dame, they formed the most frightening backfield to date for any defensive opponent to encounter.

But Thomas' and Gipp's fast friendship ended too fast, tragically. In the middle of the 1920 season, Gipp suddenly came down with a severe throat infection. Within a few weeks on December 14, 1920, Gipp died from pneumonia. Thomas was devastated.

"I broke down and cried like a baby," Thomas said during an interview years later. "It was like losing a brother."

Thomas was Rockne's quarterback from 1920 to 1922, a span that saw Thomas and his Fighting Irish teammates compile a record of 27-2-1. Rockne was captivated by Thomas' skills; he praised his quarterback as "a fine field general" to sportswriters. Following one Thomas-led Notre Dame victory, Rockne reportedly told his assistants: "It's amazing the amount of football sense that Thomas kid has. He can't miss becoming a great coach someday."

Thanks to Rockne's personal reference, Thomas had his first assistant coaching job waiting in the wings at the University of Georgia when he graduated from Notre Dame in 1923. It would take only two years cutting his teeth as an assistant before Thomas landed his first head coaching position at the University of Chattanooga.

Thomas turned Chattanooga into four seasons' worth of tough afternoons for opponents during the late 1920s. A four-year record of 26-9-2 captured the attention of the University of Alabama. When head coach Wallace Wade resigned in 1931 after establishing Alabama as a football powerhouse with three national championships, he hand-picked Thomas to take over a defending national championship team that was losing 10 of its 11 starters to graduation.

Few expectations were held out for the first-year coach with first-year starters going up against the toughest football teams the nation had to offer and a defending national championship target on Alabama's back. But Thomas's men picked up right where their predecessors left off by rolling off nine wins against only one loss and outscoring their opponents by a season-combined score of 370-57.

Thomas' Crimson Tide followed their initial season with eight wins and two losses in 1932. The next year, Alabama finished 7-1-1. Then, in 1934, Thomas's men steamrolled their way to an undefeated 10-0 season crowned by a win over Stanford in the Rose Bowl that sealed a national championship.

Among the players that helped Thomas win his first national championship as a head coach: Paul "Bear" Bryant. When Bryant graduated from Alabama in 1936, Thomas hired Bryant as an assistant and gave the future Alabama legend his first coaching job.

One of the premiere coaches in the country during an era that spanned from 1931 to 1946, Thomas guided Alabama to six bowl appearances, four of which were wins — the Rose Bowl in 1935 and 1946, the Cotton Bowl in 1942, and the Orange Bowl in 1943. However, Thomas was a heavy smoker who routinely smoked cigars on the sidelines while coaching. Health issues from heart and lung disease forced him to step down as head coach in 1946 after amassing a career record of 141-33-9.

Thomas was inducted into the College Football Hall of Fame as a coach in 1951. After leaving coaching in 1946, he stayed on at Alabama as the school's athletic director until 1952.

Thomas resigned from coaching with a career record of 141-33-9. He remained at Alabama as the school's athletic director until 1952; one year after Thomas had been inducted into the College Football Hall of Fame.

Frank William Thomas was only 55 years old when he died at Druid City Hospital in Tuscaloosa, Alabama, in 1954. Rockne's protégé was so beloved as an Alabama football legend, an illustrated book published later that year paid tribute to Thomas with his life story.

Today, the University of Alabama practice fields are named for Thomas and his 1946 successor, Harold Drew. And like his mentor, who has several statues erected in his memory, including the Rockne statue at the North Gate of Notre Dame Stadium, Thomas' bronzed likeness stands alongside the statues of Alabama's other national championship-winning coaches in the school's history - Wallace Wade, Gene Stallings, Nick Saban, and Thomas's protégé, Bear Bryant.

THE FOUR HORSEMEN

DON MILLER

• Played for Notre Dame (1922—1924), assistant for Georgia Tech (1925—1928), Ohio State (1929—1932).

Rockne's fastest Horseman had the law on his side.

Don Miller followed in the footsteps of four brothers when he left Defiance, Ohio, in 1920 and entered Notre Dame. One of his brothers, Harry "Red" Miller, had been a star halfback and team captain for the Fighting Irish whose heroics in Notre Dame's first victory over Michigan in 1909 were legendary.

Red Miller told Rockne about his speedy brother, who was running track his freshman year, and the third-year coach admitted that Miller "…surprised me when he came out for spring practice and with his fleetness and daring sized up as a halfback to cheer the heart of any coach."

The pen of Grantland Rice turned Don Miller, Elmer Layden, Jim Crowley and Harry Stuhldreher into the most storied backfield in college football history from 1922 to 1924. The lightning-fast Miller set school rushing records and, in 1923, was the lone member of the Four Horsemen to be selected to the first team All-America squad.

The following year, Layden, Crowley and Stuhldreher were all first-teamers while Miller was placed on the second team behind Illinois' Red Grange.

But Miller had other plans that stretched beyond football. After serving as president of the senior class, Miller graduated in 1925 with both a bachelor's and a law degree.

He couldn't outrun his legend as a member of the Four Horsemen on the football field, so Miller took a job as a backfield coach at Georgia Tech, a position he held from 1925 until 1928. In 1929, Miller moved to Columbus, Ohio when he landed a position as backfield coach at Ohio State University.

By 1932, Miller had had enough of football. He moved to Cleveland, and with the help of another brother, Ray T. Miller, the mayor of Cleveland and chairman of the local Democratic Party, pursued a law practice.

The fastest of the Four Horsemen went on to serve 12 years as the United States Attorney for Northern Ohio from 1941 to 1953. In 1965, Miller was appointed to the bench as a United States Bankruptcy Court judge, a federal seat he held until his retirement in 1977. He also spent a term as president of the Cuyahoga Bar Association.

The iconic Four Horseman spent the latter part of his life making frequent appearances as a speaker at football functions and Notre Dame alumni events.

The Honorable Don C. Miller died at Lakeside Hospital in Cleveland on July 28, 1979. He was 77 years old.

HARRY STUHLDREHER

• Played for Notre Dame (1922—1924), head coach for Villanova (1925—1935), Wisconsin (1936—1948).

The curly-locked kid was looking to get into Tiger Stadium in Massillon, Ohio, to see the Massillon Tigers professional football game when he spotted one of the team's stars, Knute Rockne, walking toward the entrance with a bag of gear in his hand.

"Carry yer bag, Mr. Rockne?" young Harry Stuhldreher asked.

Rockne handed his bag over to the star-struck fan on that fateful day in 1916. The sky may as well have thundered and lightning may as well have struck the Massillon ground with a bolt of football immortality. That fateful first meeting between Rockne and his future quarterback of the legendary Four Horsemen served up an omen for the first "Hail Mary" pass.

Stuhldreher grew up in Massillon, a football standout for both Massillon Washington High School and the Kiski School in Saltsburg, Pennsylvania. He graduated from the Kiski School in 1921, then headed to Notre Dame where he was a familiar face to Rockne.

Standing only 5-foot-7 and weighing a modest 150 pounds, the shifty German kid from Massillon could pass with uncanny accuracy, return punts, and block with the best of them. Most importantly in Rockne's eyes, Stuhldreher possessed a strong, self-assured leadership characteristic that made him a natural fit to take over from graduating quarterback Frank Thomas and steer the helm of a four-man backfield that already featured three of the most jaw-dropping football talents in the country: Jim Crowley, Don Miller and Elmer Layden.

"Even as a freshman, Harry had the most promise of the Four Horsemen. He sounded the leader on the field," Rockne proclaimed. By the end of his sophomore season in 1922, Stuhldreher had been entrusted by his coach to call signals on the field.

From 1922 to 1924, Stuhldreher led the Four Horsemen and Notre Dame to 27 wins, two losses (both against Nebraska in front of record crowds), and one tie. They racked up 74 points in one game in a 74-0 win over Kalamazoo in 1923, and in 1924, Stuhldreher quarterbacked the Irish to an undefeated 10-0 season that finished with a 27-10 win over Stanford in the 1925 Rose Bowl - and a national championship.

Then there was the game against Georgia Tech in 1922, a gridiron battle that clawed for every yard. Late in the game with the Irish up 6-3 and the offense faced with fourth down, Stuhldreher was set to call the play in the huddle when offensive lineman Noble Kizer suggested "a Hail Mary prayer."

Stuhldreher promptly tossed a touchdown pass to give the Irish a 13-3 victory. After the game, Kizer loudly boasted, "That Hail Mary is the best play we've got."

Rockne's field general was destined to be a coach. Almost immediately upon graduation from Notre Dame in 1925, Stuhldreher walked into the position of head coach at Villanova University.

He also moonlighted as a player, and for six games in 1926 Stuhldreher re-teamed with fellow Four Horseman Elmer Layden on the Brooklyn Horsemen of the first American Football League. When the AFL's Horsemen merged with the Brooklyn Lions of the National Football League, the first AFL, Brooklyn's NFL franchise and Stuhldreher's playing career both came to an end.

Stuhldreher stayed at Villanova for 11 seasons and compiled a respectable 65-25-9 record. In 1936, Stuhldreher moved to Madison, Wisconsin to take over as head coach and athletic director at the University of Wisconsin-Madison.

Over a span of 13 seasons at Wisconsin, Stuhldreher guided the Badgers to a 45-62-6 mark. The highlight season of Stuhldreher's Wisconsin coaching career shined in 1942. Powered by All-Americans Elroy "Crazy Legs" Hirsch, Pat Harder and Dave Schreiner, Stuhldreher's Badgers finished 8-1-1, beat top-ranked Ohio State (coached by Massillon legend Paul Brown) 17-7, and ended the season ranked third in the Associated Press poll.

The lead Horseman had plenty to fall back on outside of football. Stuhldreher — whose wife Mary was a writer — penned two books, "Knute Rockne, Man Builder," published in 1931 not long after Rockne's death, and "Quarterback Play." He also wrote a short novel, "The

Blocking Back," but it was "Knute Rockne, Man Builder" that was used as a significant reference for the film "Knute Rockne, All-American," that starred Pat O'Brien as Rockne and Ronald Reagan as George Gipp.

Stuhldreher left Wisconsin in 1948 with a career coaching record of 110-87-15. He moved to Pittsburgh and took a job at U.S. Steel in the company's industrial relations department. In 1958, Stuhldreher was elected to the College Football Hall of Fame.

Harry Augustus Stuhldreher remained in Pittsburgh until his death from acute pancreatitis on January 26, 1965. The quarterback of Notre Dame's legendary Four Horsemen was 63 years old.

JIM CROWLEY

• Played for Notre Dame (1922—1924), head coach for Michigan State (1928—1932), Fordham (1933—1941).

Droopy eyes got him tagged as the "Sleepy" member of Knute Rockne's most famous backfield, but Jim Crowley was wide awake when he lit up a dynamic three-year career running the ball as a member of Notre Dame's legendary "Four Horsemen."

Born in Chicago and raised in Green Bay where he starred at Green Bay East High School under coach Curly Lambeau, "Sleepy Jim" Crowley turned professional after graduating from Notre Dame in 1925 — both as a player and a coach.

Shortly after signing on as an assistant coach at the University of Georgia, Crowley hit the field as a halfback appearing in just three games for: first, the National Football League's Green Bay Packers, the Providence Steamrollers, and, finally, the Waterbury Blues.

Waterbury reunited Crowley with his fellow ex-Horsemen, Harry Stuhldreher, to field two of college football's most illustrious heroes to date against a team from Adams, Massachusetts. The Two Horsemen didn't disappoint: Crowley ran for three touchdowns and Stuhldreher booted two field goals and three extra points to power a 34-0 blowout.

Immediately after the game, Crowley picked up his check and walked away from the playing field.

He returned to Georgia on the sidelines, where he served as an assistant coach until 1929 when Crowley landed the job as head coach at Michigan State College, later known as Michigan State University. In four seasons, Crowley's Spartans launched their coach's epic coaching career with 22 wins, 8 losses and 3 ties.

Fordham University called in 1933. "Sleepy Jim" may have been a star of the offense as a player molded by perhaps the greatest offensive innovator in the history of the game, but as head coach at Fordham, Crowley built one of the top defensive teams in the country by 1936. A stout defensive line coached by Crowley's fellow Irish alum Frank Leahy became known as the "Seven Blocks of Granite," led by two-time All-American lineman and future Pro Football Hall of Famer Alex Wojciechowicz, and another future Pro Football Hall of Famer who would later share a Green Bay connection with Crowley — Vince Lombardi.

The first football game to be televised featured Crowley's Fordham Rams thrashing the Waynesburg Yellow Jackets, 34-7. His final two squads each went to bowl games: Fordham lost to Texas A&M, 13-12, in the 1941 Cotton Bowl Classic, then beat Missouri, 2-0, the following year in the 1942 Sugar Bowl.

Crowley left football to serve with the United States Navy in the South Pacific during World War II. In the Navy he still found time to coach the North Carolina Pre-Flight School "Cloudbusters" to a record of 8-2-1.

Following his discharge, Crowley returned to the States and agreed to become the first commissioner of the All-America Football Conference, a new professional league set to rival the National Football League.

He stepped down as commissioner at the end of the 1946 season to become part-owner of the AAFC's worst team, the Chicago Rockets. But Crowley's magic as a college head coach failed to rub off on the pros. The Rockets finished just 1-13 in 1947, and Crowley quit football for good just before the kickoff of the 1948 season.

Crowley moved to Pennsylvania and became an insurance salesman. In 1953, he took over as station manager and sports director of the independent television station WTVU in Scranton.

Two years later, Crowley was named chairman of the Pennsylvania State Athletic Commission, a position he maintained until 1963. After being named to the College Football Hall of Fame in 1966, Crowley was able to live the rest of his life cashing in on his legend as a highly sought-after speaker on the banquet and dinner circuits.

James Harold "Sleepy Jim" Crowley was the last living member of the Four Horsemen when he died in Scranton on January 15, 1986.

ELMER LAYDEN

• Played for Notre Dame (1922—1924), head coach for Duquesne (1927—1933), Notre Dame (1934—1940)

When you hear the "Star Spangled Banner" before a National Football League game, think of Elmer Layden.

Of all the players who emerged from Knute Rockne's indomitable football system at Notre Dame, it was the speedy 160-pound fullback who ran alongside Harry Stuhldreher, Jim Crowley and Don Miller as a member of the immortal Four Horsemen backfield that carried his fabled mentor's torch into Notre Dame coaching infamy.

Born in Davenport, Iowa, Layden's offensive accomplishments with the Four Horsemen earned him All-American honors his senior season in 1924 and overshadowed slick defensive skills Layden flashed on the other side of the ball. Most noteworthy were two interceptions Layden ran back for touchdowns in Notre Dame's 27-10 victory over Stanford in the 1925 Rose Bowl, his final collegiate game.

After graduating from Notre Dame, Layden played one season of professional football with a team made up of former college football stars. In one game, Layden was reunited with his fellow Notre Dame backfield icons by the

Hartford Blues who paid $5,000 for the Four Horsemen to play against the Cleveland Bulldogs. Hartford not only lost money paying the quartet for their services, the team lost the game, 13-6.

Layden hung up his spikes in 1926 for a coaching job at Loras College in Dubuque, Iowa. The next year he moved to Pittsburgh to take over the coaching helm at Duquesne. In seven years at Duquesne, Layden's teams racked up a 48-16-6 record, and capped off the 1933 season by winning the Festival of Palms Bowl, the precursor to today's Orange Bowl.

The Festival of Palms bowl win on New Year's Day 1934 was Layden's final victory at Duquesne. Three years after Rockne was killed in a plane crash on March 31, 1931, Notre Dame brought Layden back to take on the dual role of head football coach and athletic director.

Layden helped to restore the Irish to college football prominence that had diminished in the three years after Rockne's death. Over the next seven years, Layden's teams won 47 games, lost 13 and tied 3 times, and the comeback rally to defeat Ohio State 18-13 in 1935 was viewed as one of the greatest wins in Notre Dame history. The Irish finished 8-1 in 1938, losing only to rival USC in the season finale which cost them a consensus national championship, but Layden's team was still named national champions by the Dickinson System.

Nobody mistook Layden's easygoing manner for Rockne's fiery presence. But like Rockne, Layden took it upon himself to serve as a goodwill ambassador for Notre Dame.

One of Layden's most significant acts involved healing a decades-old rift between Notre Dame and Michigan. The two schools had not met on a football field since 1909, a year before Michigan had cancelled their scheduled game in 1910 and refused to play the Irish again.

Because of Layden's efforts as athletic director, Notre Dame and Michigan met again in 1942 and 1943, after Frank Leahy succeeded Layden as Notre Dame head coach. The 1943 game ended in a one-sided Irish thrashing of Michigan 35-12. Wolverine coach and athletic director Fritz Crisler was so upset over Leahy running up the score, Crisler refused to schedule the Irish again.

After taking over a Notre Dame football program that had suffered from sagging ticket sales since Rockne's death, Layden was appointed commissioner of the NFL in 1941 and left the Notre Dame athletic program with football ticket receipt totals that had nearly doubled since he took over.

Layden guided the NFL through the World War II years, a span that saw teams using many players with inferior professional football skills while the game's regulars were fighting in the war. Layden allowed some teams, most notably the Pittsburgh Steelers and the Philadelphia Eagles, to merge due to lack of manpower, and he once conducted an investigation into a betting scam without advising the owners.

Once the war was over, Commissioner Layden called on all of the league's teams to play "The Star-Spangled Banner" before the kickoff. "The National Anthem should be as much a part of every game as the kickoff," Layden proclaimed. "We must not drop it simply because the war is over. We should never forget what it stands for."

Layden served as NFL commissioner until January 1946. He left the NFL and embarked on a successful business career, first as president of the Shipper Car Line Corporation in New York, and later in the railroad equipment business with the General American Transportation Corporation of Chicago.

The legendary Four Horseman was inducted as a charter member into the College Football Hall of Fame in 1951.

Elmer Francis Layden died June 30, 1973, at the age of 70.

NOBLE KIZER

• Played for Notre Dame (1922—1924), head coach for Purdue (1930—1936)

Noble "Nobe" Kizer was one of Rockne's vaunted "Seven Mules" blocking the way for the legendary "Four Horsemen."

Born in the Indiana countryside near LaPorte, Kizer came to Notre Dame in 1921 and by his sophomore year in 1922, he had earned the starting spot at right guard as part of the Fighting Irish's offensive line, the Seven Mules, blocking for Stuhldreher, Miller, Layden and Crowley during one of college football's most historic periods.

After graduating from Notre Dame, Kizer took a job as assistant coach at Purdue under another former Rockne protégé, James Phelan. When Phelan left Purdue for a heading coaching position at the University of Washington, Kizer inherited the reins as Purdue's head coach. During his six-year span at Purdue from 1930 to 1936, Kizer guided the Boilermakers to two Big Ten Conference championships and compiled an outstanding record of 42-13-3.

Kizer also served as Purdue's athletic director from 1933 until his death on June 13, 1940 as a result of a kidney ailment and high blood pressure. Noble Earl "Nobe" Kizer Sr. died at the age of 40 years old.

CHUCK COLLINS

• Played for Notre Dame (1922—1924), head coach for North Carolina (1926 - 1933)

Perhaps it was Knute Rockne's immortal influence that persuaded Chuck Collins to put off a law career and go into coaching football after he graduated with a degree in law from Notre Dame in 1925.

A native of Chicago, Collins played left end for Rockne from 1922 to 1924, one of the vaunted "Seven Mules" blocking for the legendary "Four Horsemen" on the Irish's undefeated national championship team in 1924.

Collins once explained his decision to sidestep law and go right into football: "At Notre Dame, I didn't even have a nickel for a cup of coffee. I went there on a basketball scholarship, but I couldn't even make the freshman team. After I graduated, I was able to make $5,000 for five months of coaching football."

Instead of joining the ranks of Clarence Darrow and William Jennings Bryant, Collins stayed the football course set by Rockne. His first job took him to Chattanooga to serve as assistant line coach. But it wasn't long before Rockne's former Mule landed the head coach's job at the University of North Carolina at Chapel Hill in 1926. Collins remained head coach of the Tar Heels from 1926 to 1933, and compiled a record of 38-31-9.

Collins left North Carolina - and football - in 1934. He took a position at National Carloading in Chicago, and settled into a career with a freight-forwarding firm that would vault the former Notre Dame football star to the position of company president in 1957. When Collins' company went through a merger in 1962, he stayed on as executive vice president of the Universal Carloading and Distributing Company until he retired in 1965.

Retirement wasn't exactly in the plan. At the age of 62, Collins passed the New Jersey bar examination. For the next 10 years Collins practiced law out of his office in Ridgewood, a village in northern New Jersey where he also served as village attorney from 1967 to 1970.

Charles C. Collins died in Ridgewood, N.J. on April 14, 1977. The Rockne protege forever renowned as one of Notre Dame's legendary Seven Mules was 73 years old.

JOE BACH

• Played for Notre Dame (1923—1924), head coach for Duquesne (1934), Pittsburgh Pirates/Steelers (1935—1936; 1952—1953)

He was one of Knute Rockne's famed "Seven Mules" who blocked the way for the legendary Four Horsemen, and in the end, Joe Bach took a page out of his mentor's playbook to turn his NFL team around.

As a senior on Notre Dame's 1924 national title team — the first Irish team to win a championship — Joe Bach played a magnificent role in the Irish's first and only Rose Bowl trip in January 1925, blowing holes open for the Four Horsemen backfield as a member of one of college football's most prolific offensive lines ever, "The Seven Mules."

Ten years later, Bach was named head coach of the NFL's Pittsburgh Pirates, a team he would lead in 1935 to its best record to date with 4 wins and 8 losses, and the following year to the young franchise's first non-losing campaign with a record of 6-6.

Bach left Pittsburgh after the 1936 season and went back to coach in the college ranks. He returned to Pittsburgh in 1951 to coach the renamed Steelers, a team that had floundered for years running a single wing formation. Bach installed a T-formation offense similar to the one Rockne ran with the Seven Mules and the Four Horsemen at Notre Dame. Pittsburgh finished the 1952 season with 5 wins and 7 lessons, then followed up in 1953 with a record of 6-6.

But after three home losses to begin the preseason in 1954, Bach resigned during training camp and left the team. Bach would move on to work as a state labor mediator while he continued his football career as a scout for the Steelers.

Moments after a banquet luncheon in his honor concluded in October 1966, Joseph Anthony Bach collapsed and died. He was 65.

REX ENRIGHT

• Played for Notre Dame (1923—1925), head coach for South Carolina (1938—1942; 1946—1955).

Rex Enright served as living proof as to how great Rockne's teams during the era of the Four Horsemen and the blocking Seven Mules.

Born in Rockford, Illinois, Enright entered Notre Dame in 1922, the year Rockne devised perhaps the Fighting Irish's most potent offensive lineup of his 13-year career as head coach - a starting backfield lineup that featured Harry Stuhldreher at quarterback, Jim Crowley at left halfback, Don Miller at right halfback, and Elmer Layden at fullback. Enright was the backup fullback behind Layden in 1922, then returned to the football team in 1925 to claim the starting fullback position.

Enright was also a standout basketball player who started all four seasons for the Notre Dame basketball team from 1922 to 1926. Upon graduation from Notre Dame, Enright returned to football and played professionally for the Green Bay Packers for two seasons.

A coaching career in both sports took Enright south during the early 1930s. He first took a job as assistant football coach at the University of North Carolina in Chapel Hill, then relocated to Georgia in 1931 where he doubled as head basketball coach and assistant football coach at the University of Georgia until 1938.

Enright left Georgia in 1938 to become head football coach and athletic director at the University of South Carolina, where he would eventually leave an indelible mark on the football history of the school, and what would be formed as the Atlantic Coach Conference.

Enright also coached the South Carolina basketball squad for two seasons before he joined the United States Navy in 1943. Sporting a rank of lieutenant, Enright served in the Navy working in the Navy's athletic program in the United States. After returning to South Carolina in 1946, Enright resumed his role as head football coach, and remained on the Gamecocks sidelines until 1955 when health issues forced him to resign.

Enright, who in 1953 was credited as being one of the "ring leaders" who helped in the formation of the Atlantic Coast Conference, stayed on as South Carolina's athletic director until 1960. Although his career record of 82-62 as basketball coach at South Carolina was far more impressive than his 64-69-7 mark as the school's head football coach, Enright left coaching as South Carolina's all-time winningest football coach until Steve Spurrier bested his mark in 2011.

Rex Edward Enright, who would be inducted into the South Carolina Athletic Hall of Fame, died April 6, 1960, as a result of peptic ulcers and a rheumatic heart. He was 59 years old.

FRANK LEAHY

• Played for Notre Dame (1928—1930), head coach for Boston College (1939—1940), Notre Dame (1941—1943; 1946—1953).

At the end of the 1930 season after Notre Dame had beaten USC in the final game to win their second consecutive national championship, Knute Rockne took an injured Irish lineman with him to Minneapolis "for company" when he checked into the Mayo Clinic.

Coach and student lay in adjoining hospital beds for two weeks talking football; Rockne was being treated for phlebitis in his leg, and the player had surgery to repair torn knee ligaments. During that time, Rockne mentioned to a friend that he wanted him to meet the player, a young offensive tackle named Frankie Leahy.

"The reason I want you to meet him," Rockne reasoned, "is that someday he will be recognized as the greatest football coach of all time."

Only Rockne stands in the way of his own prophecy: Today, nearly a century later, Rockne and Leahy rank No. 1 and No. 2 among Division I coaches with the highest all-time winning percentage in college football history. Born in O'Neill, Nebraska, it's only fitting that the coach with the second highest winning percentage in college football history grew up in the town of Winner, South Dakota, where he was a standout football player at Winner High School.

The friend replied by asking Rockne what was so exceptional about young Leahy. "That kid has the greatest football brain I have ever come in contact with," Rockne gushed. "He is just simply genius when it comes to planning ways and means of getting that ball across the goal line and smothering the play of the opponents. Take it from me, he is a super-strategist already."

If not for a knee injury that sidelined him for the final season of his Irish playing career, Leahy would have anchored the offensive line at left tackle for Rockne's last three teams, including the 1929 and 1930 championship squads. That injury turned out to be a fateful blessing for Leahy, who sat on the bench during games with Rockne and soaked up knowledge directly from the master that laid the foundation for a brilliant future coaching career.

Leahy graduated from Notre Dame in 1931. He immediately landed his first assistant coaching job at Georgetown. During a game against Notre Dame legend Jim Crowley's Michigan State team, Crowley was so impressed by Georgetown's line work under the rookie assistant, he recruited Leahy to join his staff at Michigan State in 1932.

Leahy's tenure at Michigan State lasted only one year. The following season, Crowley was hired to be the new head coach at Fordham, and Leahy followed Crowley to New York City to take on the task of Fordham's offensive line coach. From 1935 to 1937, Leahy's linemen were so dominant, they were tagged the "Seven Blocks of Granite" by the press. Included among the Seven of Blocks of Granite was a tough kid who would go on to become perhaps the NFL's greatest head coach — Vince Lombardi.

By 1939, Leahy moved on again, this time to take the helm of his own team at Boston College. In just two seasons, Leahy guided the Eagles to a 20-2 record, including an undefeated national championship season in 1940 that was capped with a victory in the 1941 Sugar Bowl. One of the players Leahy tried to recruit to Boston College was future beat author Jack Kerouac, a promising high school standout from Lowell, Massachusetts who wound up going to Columbia University.

In the wake of his undefeated championship season of 1940, Leahy turned down offers from three different schools, one of which would have set him up financially for life, to sign a new five-year contract and stay at Boston College. But a mere 24 hours after Leahy put his signature on a deal that would keep him with the Eagles for at least five more years, he got a call from his alma mater with an offer to return as Irish head coach.

Leahy jumped at the offer to coach the team his mentor had built, but Boston College wasn't about to tear up his contract before the ink of Leahy's signature had dried. Despite Leahy's pleas to the school's vice president, the mayor of Boston, and the governor of Massachusetts, he took his case in front of a press conference and announced: "Gentlemen, I've called you all here today to inform you that I recently received my release from my coaching contract. With the release went the good wishes and benediction of Boston College."

The South Bend Tribune called Leahy's announcement, "the biggest lie of his life." But as soon as Leahy had stepped away from the podium, a call came in from the vice president of Boston College. "Coach Leahy," the school's VP snarled, "you may go wherever you want, and whenever you want. Goodbye."

By the time Leahy returned to Notre Dame as head coach for the 1941 season, he had grown into his own man with his own methods and innovations. Any similarities between Leahy and Rockne were few and far between. Leahy, like Rockne, was a stubborn perfectionist who paid strict attention to every detail. And, like Rockne, Leahy won football games at an astounding rate with coaching innovations and strategies that nobody else in the college ranks came close to.

Among Leahy's most significant creations included the implementation of a double-quarterback formation, having his teams run from the stand-up position, optional blocking assignments for linemen on the same running play, and formulating a pass defense against Georgia Tech during the 1941 season that was used by most NFL teams at the time.

Leahy worked his men hard, but they held a profound respect for his authority and knowledge, and they appreciated his concern for their physical well-being. Using his own knee injury that sidelined him for Rockne's last season in 1930 as a barometer, Leahy was relentless in finding ways to safeguard his players from getting hurt.

Leahy left Notre Dame in 1944 to enter the U.S. Navy. For two years, Leahy served as lieutenant commander in charge of recreational programs for submarine crews. When he returned to South Bend in 1946, Notre Dame was the top-ranked team in the country. Leahy led the Irish on a 39-

game winning streak that finally came to an end in 1950 with a loss to Purdue.

In addition to the national championship his Boston College Eagles claimed in 1940, Leahy's Notre Dame teams captured four national titles — 1943, 1946, 1947 and 1949 — an unprecedented run as head coach of his alma mater that earned him the nickname, "The Master."

Health problems began to creep in on October 24, 1953, when Leahy was stricken by a pancreatic attack. Although Notre Dame was, again, ranked as the best team in the country, ill-health forced Layden to step down as Irish head coach at the end of the 1953 season.

After leaving Notre Dame, Leahy spent his time giving football game previews on radio and television shows. He struck up a business friendship with financier Louis Wolfson, and in 1955 Leahy was elected vice president for trade relations for the marine construction and salvage firm, Merritt-Chapman & Scott Corporation.

Leahy returned to football in 1960 when he was named general manager of the Los Angeles Chargers during the inaugural season of the American Football League. Three years later, Leahy moved to Portland, Oregon when he landed a job as an executive in a vending machine company.

He was inducted into the National Football Foundation Hall of Fame in 1970.

Francis William Leahy, the coach who took the lessons he learned directly from Knute Rockne and forged a legendary career in his own right that to this day stands second only to his mentor in all-time winning percentage, died from congestive heart failure in Portland on June 21, 1973. He was 64 years old.

FRANK CARIDEO

• Played for Notre Dame (1928—1930), head coach for Missouri (1932—1934)

Knute Rockne himself called Frank Carideo "...the best quarterback ever."

Born in Mount Vernon, New York, Carideo played under Rockne at Notre Dame from 1928 to 1930 and led the Irish to a perfect 19-0 record over a two-year period as a starter.

A two-time All-American, Carideo was quarterback of the last Rockne-coached Notre Dame team in 1930, a team that went undefeated and secured Notre Dame's third national championship under Rockne with a crushing win over USC in December 1930.

After graduating from Notre Dame, Carideo followed in his mentor's footsteps at Purdue where he served as an assistant coach in 1931. Carideo left Purdue to take a coaching job at the University of Missouri from 1932 to 1934. Carideo's Missouri teams went 2-23-2 during his span.

He departed Missouri after three seasons to coach basketball at Mississippi State University from 1935 to 1939. Carideo returned to football as an assistant coach at Iowa from 1939 to 1942, as well as during the 1946 and 1949 seasons.

Francis F. Carideo died in Ocean Springs, Mississippi in 1992 at the age of 83.

30

CHANGING FLIGHT

In life, Knute Rockne charted the course for the game of football.

Rockne's death may have exerted an even more profound change on the nation and perhaps the world. When his plane crashed to the ground of a Kansas farm field at about 10:45 a.m. on March 31, 1931, Rockne's death forever altered aviation in the United States and future air travel around the globe for good.

The crash on March 31, 1931 forced the Aeronautics Branch of the Department of Commerce to become more transparent because Rockne was one of the victims.

For five years, following 1926 when Herbert Hoover installed the Department of Commerce as the regulating branch of the aviation industry, federal government investigations of air crashes had been kept confidential from the press and the public. Keeping federal crash investigations secret was meant to spur the growth of the blossoming aviation industry and sell the public on the safety of air travel, while airline companies colluded in efforts to keep crashes out of the public eye by removing wreckage from sites and destroying records to thwart investigations.

The public, however, clamored for information on the crash that killed Rockne. Media pressure, which had been mounting all across the country for five years to get access to federal crash investigations, swarmed over Bazaar, Kansas, like an intense storm cloud.

Because Knute Rockne was one of the victims, the Aeronautics Branch immediately sent a federal investigation team to a plane crash site for the first time. Because of Rockne, it would be the first time the Department of Commerce released its crash investigation findings to the media for public consumption.

Three years later in 1934, Congress passed the Air Commerce Act, which gave the Department of Commerce full authority to issue subpoenas and directions to make investigations public.

The crash that claimed the life of Rockne promptly grounded the wooden Fokker F-10 Trimotor plane and killed the Fokker airline as a viable company. More importantly, Rockne's death in a wooden-structured plane spelled the end of wooden aircraft flying in commercial aviation.

Airline manufacturers immediately began the move to replace wood with metal, and the all-metal Ford Trimotor and Boeing 247 airships seized the market. T&WA, frozen out of the Boeing market by rival companies, requested specifications for an all-new metal airliner from Douglas Aircraft. Within one year, Douglas developed the DC-1/2, which would eventually become the DC-3, the most successful and long-lasting airliner in commercial aviation history until it went out of service in the early 1990s.

Rockne's legacy is etched in the DC-3's metal foundation that turned air travel from an American adventure into a worldwide business.

As impressive as the DC-3's performance and safety factors were, even more startling were the drastic decreases in cost-per-seat mile, which made air travel not only safer, but more affordable and cost-effective. The 21-seat DC-3 became the first passenger airplane to make profits for airlines without the added funds provided by transporting mail. Well over 10,000 DC-3s would be manufactured in the U.S.A., with 2,000 more built in Russia and another 500 made in Japan. The DC-3 also flew in just about every Allied air operation of World War II, and served as a significant military air tool in both the Korean and Vietnam wars.

Granted, had the Rockne crash never happened and the legendary coach gone on to a long and unprecedented head coaching career at Notre Dame, the aviation industry would have progressed away from three-engine wooden airliners flying at 120 miles per hour. It's just that the development of the metal airliner would have been different, evidenced by the clunky, slow Junkers manufactured in the mid-1930s.

If not for the ambitious airline manufacturing market created by the Rockne crash, Douglas would not have built the DC-3, considered to this day to be the aviation industry's pioneering masterpiece. Perhaps worldwide air travel would have developed more slowly without the DC-3 and its passenger-friendly economy, safety and comfort. As well, there may have been slower acceptance of the high-performance military monoplanes and civil-service airplanes.

But Rockne did die in a plane crash.

And the aviation industry memorialized his incredible life by moving to right the wrongs of the airliner in which he was killed and to make aviation travel safer, technologically progressive, and more transparent for the public's consumption.

31

IN MEMORIAL

In a message to Mrs. Rockne, President Herbert Hoover wrote: "I know that every American grieves with you. Mr. Rockne so contributed to a cleanness and high purpose and sportsmanship in athletics that his passing is a national loss."

Rockne's legacy lives in memorials across the country and around the globe — from his home in Norway to the continent of Australia — befitting not only a legendary football coach, but a true national treasure on the level of a president, a king, a fallen national hero.

Artist Jerry McKenna has no peer when it comes to sculpting memorial busts and statues of Knute Rockne. The Boerne, Texas-based sculptor, a 1962 graduate of Notre Dame, has crafted a total of 11 Rockne statues.

Among McKenna's prominent Rockne works include: the statue on the north end of Notre Dame Stadium; a statue of Rockne in downtown South Bend; the Rockne bust in the Notre Dame football team's locker room; a memorial statue in Rockne's birthplace of Voss, Norway; a statue in the town of Rockne, Texas; a bust at the Matfield Green travel plaza on the Kansas Turnpike eight miles from the crash site near Bazaar, Kansas; a bust at the Cottonwood Falls Museum in Cottonwood Falls, Kansas, the closest town to the crash; a bust in the Guglielmino Athletics Complex - "The Gug," — that houses the football practice locker rooms, coaches' offices and meeting rooms on the campus of Notre Dame; and, perhaps most appropriately, a bust in the office of current Notre Dame football coach Brian Kelly.

Capturing the expressive grin on Rockne's face on the statue outside Notre Dame Stadium is a testament to McKenna's spiritual kinship with the legendary coach.

"I gotta be honest..." McKenna says, pausing to collect his artistic perception of a muse so personally beloved.

"All I want is to sculpt a masterpiece, and I fall short... Even though he's got very unique features, he's been very difficult to sculpt over the years. I've done hundreds of portrait busts, but I just find him very different to capture; it took a very long time to do the pieces. I was a bit inhibited because I held him in such awe. I just couldn't get over that, and I probably still haven't."

A marble and limestone memorial monument honoring Rockne and the five other passengers, pilot and co-pilot was erected at the site of the crash in Chase County, Kansas, a sprawling 1,539-acre plot of open pasture on the edge of the Flint Hills previously owned by the family estate of witness Easter Heathman. When the property was sold at auction for more than $4 million in February 2018, the auction company told the Kansas City Star that the Rockne memorial marked the land with "a little more character."

On March 29, 2019, two days before the 88th anniversary of the crash, the Rockne Memorial was officially dedicated at the Matfield Green travel plaza on the Kansas Turnpike. McKenna's bust of Rockne is the featured display at the newest memorial site located about eight miles north of the crash site.

In the wake of the crash in 1931, the children of Sacred Heart School in the small farming community of Hilbigville, Texas, were given the opportunity to choose a name for their town. The kids voted to rename the town, Rockne, to honor the fallen coach. On March 10, 1988, the town of Rockne opened its first post office and issued a commemorative, 22-cent Rockne stamp. On March 4, 2006, a life-size bust of Rockne was unveiled in the town.

In Allentown, Pennsylvania, the gymnasium inside Allentown Central Catholic High School is named Rockne Hall. The street next to the football field in Taylorville, Illinois., is called Knute Rockne Road. South Bend, and Stevensville, Michigan, where Rockne had a summer home, also have streets named after the legendary coach. A gas and food stop on the Indiana Toll Road not far from South Bend is called the Knute Rockne Travel Plaza.

Soon after his death, the Studebaker automobile company in South Bend began building the Rockne model automobile, a manufacturing project priced to sell in a low-cost market during the early years of the Great Depression.

Rockne also became the subject of various music and film releases that began shortly after the plane crash. In 1931, the year that Rockne died, composer Ferde Grofe, whose credits include the Grand Canyon Suite and Rip Van Winkle, penned a symphonic musical suite to honor Rockne.

Perhaps the most famous film tribute came in 1940 with the Warner Brothers release of "Knute Rockne, All American," starring actor Pat O'Brien who recreated the famous locker scene in which Rockne used the phrase, "win one for the Gipper." Young actor Ronald Reagan portrayed George Gipp in the film, and later used the phrase during one of his speeches after he had been elected president.

The 1944 film short, "I Am an American," also featured Rockne as a foreign-born American citizen. Most recently in 2008, a biographical musical of Rockne's life based on a play and mini-series penned by Buddy Farmer hit the stage at the Theatre at the Center in Munster, Indiana.

Rockne was enshrined as a charter member of the College Football Hall of Fame in 1951, as well as the Indiana Football Hall of Fame. He was also inducted posthumously into the Scandinavian-American Hall of Fame held during Norsk Horstfest. Rockne was also inducted into the Rose Bowl Hall of Fame in 2014.

The U.S. Navy memorialized Rockne in 1943 by naming a ship the SS Knute Rockne. Rockne's face was also featured on a stamp. In 1988, President Ronald Reagan appeared at Notre Dame's Athletic & Convocation Center to give a speech and unveil the U.S. Postal Service's 22-cent Rockne commemorative postage stamp the same day it was released in Rockne, Texas.

The Knute Rockne Memorial Building also stands as a Notre Dame honorarium to Rockne. Built in 1939 with funding by donations from alumni and friends of the University, "The Rock" still stands as one of the most complete recreational facilities on campus for students, facility, staff, retirees and their families.

"The Rock" features a lower-level exercise room and weight room, a 25-yard swimming pool and warm-up pool with observation decks, racquetball and squash courts, plus locker rooms for men, women and families — a bustling facility for club sports, intramurals, fitness classes, aquatic instruction and life-saving classes. The upper level includes a gymnasium complete with two basketball courts.

The main lobby of "The Rock" stands as a true memorial to the legendary coach. Athletic trophies and mementos accumulated by Notre Dame teams under Rockne and his successors are displayed, as well as a bronze bust of Rockne that greets patrons and campus visitors. Students have turned the Rockne bust into a long-standing source of tradition by rubbing Rockne's nose for good luck.

32

THE HOUSE THAT

ROCKNE BUILT

His most magnificent and enduring legacy sits as the

football centerpiece of the University of Notre Dame —
Notre Dame Stadium.

By 1928, Notre Dame under Rockne had become such
a national football powerhouse, a mediocre 5-4 season did
little to dim net profits that soared to nearly $500,000. The
team was getting way too popular to handle crowds that
packed into the campus's smaller Cartier Field. A new
stadium was in the planning stages; however, Holy Cross
priests were dragging their feet on decisions that needed to
be made to allocate money to build a new stadium.

Rockne grew increasingly frustrated with the delays, which were complicated by a variety of additional issues. Finally, chomping at the bit for a new stadium, yet armed with offers on the table from a handful of universities that promised richer annual salaries to coach their football teams and turn their schools into a national cash cow, Rockne submitted his resignation to the university's president, Father O'Donnell.

But Father O'Donnell knew that excess receipts from the 1928 season, plus projected receipts generated by playing all away games in 1929 on neutral fields, could adequately finance the construction of the new stadium without putting the university in debt. Father O'Donnell could also offer a tempting caveat — allow Rockne input as to how he would like the new stadium to be designed.

Rockne was good to stay at Notre Dame and mold the new stadium in his own vision.

Working with Osborn Engineering of Cleveland, the firm that had designed both Yankee Stadium and Boston's Fenway Park, Rockne used the University of Michigan Stadium as a model. At a final cost of $750,000, the original Notre Dame Stadium was a smaller-scale version of Michigan Stadium, with space between the playing field and the stands cut to a minimum.

The main difference between the two was the location of the tunnel, which was opened on the north end of Notre Dame Stadium. Today, the Knute Rockne Gate where both Notre Dame players and the visiting team, plus the marching band and all cheerleaders enter for games, is marked by the iconic bronze Rockne statue.

Notre Dame Stadium opened its gates on Oct. 4, 1930, holding a capacity of 59,075 people. That debut season, which ended with Rockne's Irish capturing their third and final national championship under his helm, would be the only season Knute Rockne coached football in the stadium he designed.

Today, the original bowl of Rockne's view sits under the massive steel framework of two nine-story buildings added to the stadium as part of Notre Dame University's $400 million Campus Crossroads project. An additional six-story building is also being built on the stadium's south end. The field's natural grass was replaced by field turf in 2014. What began as a stadium that seated nearly 60,000 today boasts a capacity of 80,795.

While towering new construction, field turf, added press boxes and stadium suites overwhelm the view from the outside that once stood as a stark centerpiece of college football tradition in the massive surrounding parking lot, they have done little to diminish the old-school tradition of Notre Dame football.

The stadium sits at 2010 Moose Krause Circle. Statues of legendary Irish coaches greet fans entering each of the stadium gates: Dan Devine at Gate A; Ara Parseghian at Gate B; Frank Leahy at Gate C; Lou Holtz at Gate D — all Hall of Fame inductees, all having won at least one national championship at Notre Dame.

But there's only one Rockne Gate.

One "House That Rockne Built."

One statue with a cocked head to the side standing with the slightest grin of a football Mona Lisa that seems to encourage every passerby to make his next step just a little bit better than the last.

One life that shaped the football, perfected the forward pass, brainstormed the shifting offense, stacked the box on defense, took college teams coast to coast, forged lasting rivalries with reverence and respect, promoted Notre Dame as a national tradition, sold the game into a showtime of financial fortune... and won one for the Gipper.

Knute Rockne defined an era. He personified life in shoulder pads. In death, he dictated the future of aviation safety. There are countless memorials, tributes and lasting memories carried on into the afterlife by the people who knew him and the people who handed down their personal memories to their children, their grandchildren, and their grandchildren's children.

But to this day, and every day as long as there's life, just as there is only one football used in play during the game, there remains only one...

Knute Rockne — a man who became a legend.

Acknowledgments

This book would not have been possible without the immeasurable contributions of time, resources and expertise generously gifted by an incredible group of people.

My huge debt of gratitude goes out to John Bybee, whose ceaseless supply of reference works, official documents and knowledge of aviation history guided me profoundly throughout the flight of this phenomenal story. Jim Managan, Father John Reynolds' direct matriarchal descendant, graciously granted access to the cassette tapes of the last interview given by Father Reynolds. Because of Jim's generosity, this storyline is drawn directly from the tape-recorded voice of the only actual eyewitness to the Jake Lingle murder.

Blessings of appreciation to Father Richard Layton at Our Lady of Guadalupe Abbey, and to Ron Karten, for sharing candid and entertaining personal insights that make this book as much of a testament to Father Reynolds' mortal truth as it does to the football truth of Knute Rockne.

A warm heart extends to Jim "Augie" Augustine, a true blue-and-gold Notre Dame community institution, chief shopkeeper of Augie's Locker Room in South Bend, and provider of unrequited moral support on countless occasions.

I am proud to include Jerry McKenna's artistic insights into the brilliant memorials he has sculpted in Coach Rockne's image. Thank you, Jerry, for your art that will keep the spirit of Knute Rockne alive forever. Your presence lends an indelible majesty to this book.

Special thanks to Lesley Martin and Katie Levi at Chicago History Museum. They made tracking down some rare, historical photographs a completely hassle-free, friendly exploration of Chicago.

Thank you, Craig Pinkus, for the legal consultation and the many years of friendship. Thanks also to Bill Jonas for the steady guidance, and for sticking as a buddy for too many years to admit. To Dan Reutebuch, my lifelong Tippecanoe River brother, there aren't enough bro-hugs in the world to express my gratitude.

It was an honor to work with Kerry Temple and John Nagy at Notre Dame Magazine. The faith Kerry put in me to write THAT story and nail it down for the Notre Dame audience is too overwhelming for words. This book strives to meet the same high standards and dedication to integrity that graces Notre Dame Magazine under Kerry Temple's leadership. All my love and appreciation to Hedy, my soul mate, my best friend. Without her unconditional support, I would have been lost in the wind instead of a writer on a mission to put out the greatest story that ever found my pen.

To Rochelle Day, Georges Toumayan, Richard Ryan and Dr. Len Clark, thank you for making one hell of a team. Spiritual blessings go out to the memory of Dorothy Corson, "The Spirit of Notre Dame" herself who lit the first match on the Father Reynolds story in her online blog on March 31, 2003.

Lastly, to my dearly departed soul brother, Neil Raabe, the greatest Notre Dame football fan I'll ever know... bless you for siding up to Knute Rockne in heaven and talking him in to throwing me the greatest pass I've ever caught.

J.G.H., March 31, 2020

SOURCE INDEX

PROLOGUE

"Rockne of Notre Dame"
Delos W. Lovelace
G.P. Putnam's Sons
1931

Shake Down The Thunder: The Official Biography of Frank Leahy
Wells Twombley
Chilton Book Company; Radnor, Pennsylvania
1974

The New York Times — Oct. 30, 1929
"Rockne's Condition Pronounced Worse; Notre Dame
Coach Must Forego Trips With Team
Perhaps for Rest of Season. Leg Injury Aggravated His
Journey to Carnegie Tech Game in Defiance
of Physicians' Orders Causes Relapse."

The Tampa Daily News
"Rockne Sick And Weary After Record Grid Campaign" -
Dec. 11, 1930

"Rockne Warned To Quit Strenuous Life" - Dec. 23, 1930

The Art of Manliness — artofmanliness.com — June 26, 2008
"Lessons in Manliness: Knute Rockne"

Newspapers.com

Moberly Monitor — (Moberly, Missouri) — Wednesday, June 11, 1930

The Daily Times (Davenport, Iowa) - Wednesday, April 1, 1931
"Hoover Leads Nation in Mourning Rockne"
"Fighting Spirit of Notre Dame is Crushed by Death"
"Funeral May Be Delayed Until April 8"

The Daily Times (Davenport, Iowa) - Thursday, April 2, 1931
"Weather And Human Element Blamed by Fokker For Crash"
Chicago Daily Tribune - Wednesday, April 1, 1931
"Thousands Will Pay Tribute to Football Chief"
"Defense Ends Testimony for Leo Brothers"

The Indianapolis News - Wednesday, April 1, 1931
"Thousands Mourn Passing of Rockne As Tributes Come From All Parts Of World"
"Coaches, Players Pay Tribute To Rockne As Coaching Genius"

"Rockne's Death Reveals His Many - Sided Career"

New York Daily News - Wednesday, April 1, 1931
"Knute Rockne And 7 Others Killed As Plane Crashes"
"Rockne Wire Gets To Wife After Crash"
"Tragedy Dazes All Notre Dame And South Bend"

The Boston Globe - Wednesday, April 1, 1931
"Mrs. Rockne On Her Way Home"
"Rockne's Sons Fight Against Their Grief"
"Leo Leary Tells About His Friend Rockne: Describes His
Hold On Players, His Storytelling, And
His Use of Psychology"
"Among The First To Identify Rockne"
"State Ends Lingle Case"
"Rockne Became Catholic in 1925"
"Rockne Had Said Death Might As Well Strike In Plane As
Elsewhere"
"Refused at First to Believe Knute Had Been Killed"
"'Pop' Warner and 'Navy Bill' Ingram Told of Tragedy
Upon Leaving Plane"
"Joked About Landings On Eve of Tragedy"

**The Tampa Times (Tampa, Florida) — Wednesday,
April 1, 1931**
"Knute Rockne Death Crash Investigated: Coroner Would
Learn Cause of Wreck of Air Liner"
Great Falls Tribune (Great Falls, Montana) - Thursday,
April 2, 1931

"Cause of Tragic Airplane Crash Remains Mystery: Nearly
Score of Witnesses Are Quizzed"
The Brownsville Herald (Brownsville, Texas) — Thursday,
April 2, 1931
"Mystery today surrounded the disappearance of $55,000
which H.J. Christen, Chicago
businessman, withdrew from his bank shortly before
starting on the airplane journey…"

The Times (Munster, Indiana) — Friday, April 3, 1931
"Pay Respect To Rockne"

The Indianapolis Star — April 5, 1931
"Pilot Fry Buried"

The People v. Brothers 180 N.E. 442
Illinois Supreme Court Justice Norman L. Jones
Illinois Supreme Court - Feb. 19, 1932

My Al Capone Museum
"Jake Lingle"
myalcaponemuseum.com

American Hauntings
"Who Killed Jake Lingle"
americanhauntingsink.com

"Made In Hollywood"
James Bacon
1977

Father John Reynolds taped interview — January 1986
By Ron Karten for Catholic Sentinel (Portland, Oregon)
Interview conducted at Our Lady of Guadalupe Abbey in
Lafayette, Oregon

Catholic Sentinel (Portland, Oregon) — Feb. 7, 1986
"Famed Trappist Dies at 91"
Ron Karten

"Who Killed Jake Lingle?"
American Hauntings - americanhauntingsink.com

Official Crash Investigation Report
Aeronautics Branch of the U.S. Department of Commerce
Filed: April 15, 1931

The Catholic Key Online
"Knute Rockne, Still Remembered After All These Years"
by Marty Denzer

Shake Down The Thunder: The Creation of Notre Dame Football
Murray Sperber
2002
"The One-Way Ride"
Walter Noble Burns
Doubleday, Doran & Company
1931

"Chicago Surrenders"
Edward Dean Sullivan
The Vanguard Press, New York
1930

**Scarface Al and the Crime Crusaders: Chicago's
Private War Against Capone**
"In March 1931"
Jan. 4, 2008

Topeka Capital-Journal — April 8, 2004
"Other fatal plane crash often forgotten"

Prairy Erth: A Day Map
"Regarding Fokker Niner-Niner-Easy"
William Least Heat-Moon
1991

Air & Space — Dec. 1991-Jan. 1992
"The Crash That Killed Knute Rockne"
Dominick A. Pisano

FBI Records — The Vault
"1933 Crash of United Airlines Trip 23 Boeing 247
NC13304"
The Vintage Airplane — January 1989
"The Forgotten Rockne Crash"
Lt. Col. Boardman C. Reed

Flying The Line

"The First Half Century of Airline Pilots Association"
George E. Hopkins

UND.com
"The Coach Maker"
Dr. Bernie Kish
Nov. 12, 2000

Wikipedia.com
Gus Dorais

York Daily Record — Sept. 17, 1975
"Gus Dorais To Be Honored"

Pro Football Archives
"Stan Cofall"

Encyclopedia of Cleveland History
"Stan Cofall"

Wikipedia.com
"Charlie Bachman"

National Football Foundation #Football Matters
"Charlie Bachman"

CatholicAthletics.com

National Football Foundation #Football Matters
"Buck Shaw"

Wikipedia.com
"Frank Thomas"

Chicago Tribune — April 25, 2019
"Frank Thomas, Played for Knute Rockne and Coached
Bear Bryant. Soon He'll Join the Indiana
Football Hall of Fame"

Rollbamaroll.com — Nov. 18, 2009
"A Look Back at Frank Thomas"
The Desert Sun — Jan. 26, 1965
"Harry Stuhldreher, One of 4 Horsemen Dies"
The Hartford Blues Part I
Jim Hogrogian
1982

Goldenrankings.com
"A Season In Time: Notre Dame 1924"

Revolvy.com
"Harry Stuhldreher"

The New York Times — Jan. 16, 1986
"Jim Crowley, Final Member of Four Horsemen Is Dead"

Los Angeles Times — Jan. 16, 1986
"Jim Crowley Dies at 83; He was the Last of the Four
Horsemen"

The New York Times — July 1, 1973
"Elmer Layden Dead"

Und.com
"Elmer Layden"

The New York Times — July 30, 1979
"Don Miller Dies at 77"

Dave's History Corner blogspot — Nov. 11, 2015
"Don Miller"

The New York Times — June 14 1940
"Noble Kizer Dies: A Football Leader"

Revolvy.com
"Noble Kizer"

###

About the Author

Jeffrey G. Harrell was born to write and create music in Indianapolis, Indiana. The proud instigator of an award-winning newspaper career that took him from Fort Lauderdale to New York City, Jeff is a professional musician, songwriter, record producer, grilling aficionado, voyeur of the natural order, a lifetime subscriber to the human condition... and a diehard fan of the Chicago Bears.

www.ingramcontent.com/pod-product-compliance
Lightning Source LLC
Chambersburg PA
CBHW060005100426
42740CB00010B/1403